Mainstreaming Sustainable Architecture
Casa de Paja: A Demonstration

Mainstreaming Sustainable Architecture
Casa de Paja: A Demonstration

Ed Paschich
Jan Zimmerman

Illustrations by Dave Madden, AIA
Photographs by Wristen Paschich
Design by The Outsource, Ltd. Co.

High Desert Press
Corrales, New Mexico

First Edition
Printed in the United States of America

ISBN 0-8263-2379-0

Published by High Desert Press
P.O. Box 1877
Corrales, New Mexico 87048 USA
505-898-6284

Acknowledgments

The authors are grateful to the many people who contributed to this book, the craftspeople who built it, and Virginia Price and Allen Heaton who enjoy living in *Casa de Paja*. In particular, we appreciate the efforts of Louis Skoler, AIA, of Syracuse, New York, and Anne Zimmerman, AIA, of AZ Architecture Studios, Santa Monica, California, for their careful reading of the text and drawings. Any errors that remain are solely those of the authors.

We owe special thanks to Dave Madden, AIA, for all the drawings; Wristen Paschich for photography; Carol Klimek of The Outsource, Ltd. for the cover and book design; and landscaper Jan Ward for the information and initial sketches on plants, drip irrigation, and xeriscaping.

Of the many people who supported this effort, several stand out: Tenley Zumwalt and Karen Schmiege of Sandia Consulting Group; Kelly Kelsey and Laura Wolf of Passage Construction; and Peter Moulson and Elizabeth Hadas of UNM Press. The City of Albuquerque, the University of Arizona, Jean-Louis Bourgeois, Jonas Lehrman, and Catherine Wanek not only generously allowed us to reprint their photographs and tables as indicated in the captions, but also made extraordinary efforts to ship us the necessary material quickly. Our thanks.

Foreword

I am an earth educator; I help people understand how the ecological systems of life work. I encourage my students to experience natural places, deepen their feelings for the earth and its life, and make decisions about their lifestyle that will lessen their impact on the planet. For instance, we all know that the food we eat contains energy – stored sunlight energy that has traveled from the sun through food chains. But we don't always realize the enormous amounts of energy, often provided by fossil fuels – another form of stored sunlight energy – that it takes to grow, process, package, and transport that food. With an increased realization of the ways that we use energy and of the ramifications of those uses in terms of pollution, global warming and so on, we can choose to act more wisely.

Casa de Paja is a tangible example of earth education. It reveals the hidden costs of building and shows the many choices we make when constructing and living in our homes. *Casa de Paja* considers far more than just the energy used in heating and cooling. It takes into account the embodied energy in the materials that were used, the impact on the environment during production of the materials, and the length of time that the materials will last until they need to be replaced. All these are important criteria for any building that claims to be sustainable.

One other thing makes *Casa de Paja* unique: it demonstrates that sustainable building practices can easily become mainstream. *Casa de Paja* is not just efficient, it is truly beautiful. Technically, a sustainable building doesn't need to have beauty, but visiting *Casa de Paja* made me realize that it can and it should. Ultimately *Casa de Paja* makes living in an environmentally friendly home more comfortable and desirable than living in a standard, energy-inefficient house.

Our society is not yet ready for sustainable building as the norm. We won't see straw bale construction, earth air conditioning, and rainwater catchment become standard in suburbia in the next few years. It is vital, though, that builders, developers and homeowners actively experiment now with a wide variety of sustainable building practices. One day in the not-too-distant future, the dwindling supply of fossil fuels, changing climates and increasing pollution will require us to adopt more sustainable practices in everything we do. When that day comes, the early lessons of *Casa de Paja* will have blazed a trail.

Bruce Johnson
International Program Coordinator, The Institute for Earth Education
Assistant Professor of Education, University of Arizona
Tucson, Arizona

TABLE OF CONTENTS

INTRODUCTION

Mainstreaming Sustainable Architecture

In New Mexico, straw bale construction has become so trendy that it's almost a cliché. Houses, post offices, courtyard walls, and roadside rest stops. Libraries, restaurants, even high-tech office parks are being built of low-tech straw. Announcing plans for a straw bale building immediately generates opinions about the straw bale house down the street. Notices for straw bale workshops are posted on bulletin boards at food co-ops and appear in continuing education catalogs. "Green builder" programs now award developers who use environmentally-sound materials like straw.

With knowing nods, local residents analyze the costs, environmental benefits, problems, and satisfactions of building with straw versus those of building with rammed earth or recycled tires. All that's missing in the endless stream of comment is a comparison to the house that Jack built! Most commentators ignore the fact that straw bales alone are not enough to make a house earth-friendly or energy-efficient.

Mainstreaming Sustainable Architecture looks at straw as only one element in a house that incorporates a variety of energy-saving, environmentally-sensitive techniques, from compacted earth subflooring to a tin roof. These approaches are loosely grouped under the term "sustainable architecture," which means choosing materials and techniques that can be maintained for the long-term without exhausting non-renewable resources.

Although most sustainable methodologies are no longer "alternative" or "experimental," they are hardly the norm in construction. But there's no reason sustainable techniques can't become standard features of any new or remodeled house. In response to an accelerating demand for environmentally friendly products over the past 10 years, manufacturers have developed more building materials that are recycled, non-polluting, and/or drawn from renewable resources. As the availability of such materials has increased, their cost has decreased.

Casa de Paja (House of Straw) illustrates a systems approach to design and construction in which the various components—such as passive solar techniques, earth air conditioning, vapor-permeable ceilings, and cellulose insulation—operate synergistically to achieve environmental goals. The house demonstrates that many elements of sustainable architecture can be incorporated without sacrificing sophisticated design and without added expense.

Some materials used in *Casa de Paja* are more expensive than conventional alternatives, but cost less to install or maintain. In other cases, the reverse is true. Overall, however, construction is cost-neutral compared to conventional housing, thus removing one frequently cited obstacle to building with sustainable techniques. Future savings from reduced energy and water consumption make sustainable architecture more economically attractive over time.

Unlike many other books, magazines, videotapes, and pamphlets about straw bale construction, this is not a "do-it-yourself" manual. Although *Mainstreaming Sustainable Architecture* is written primarily for potential homeowners who care about the earth, it is also addressed to developers, architects, and builders who accept responsibility for creating environmentally sensitive and energy-efficient houses.

While no technical background is needed to understand the principles behind sustainable design, architects and engineers will find enough detail in the drawings and appendices to adapt these techniques to their own construction. The appendices provide a wealth of information on materials, suppliers, and other resources. The most innovative features of the house are explored in depth:

- an innovative venting technique to ensure that the straw bales remain dry;
- earth air conditioning to cool (or warm) the outside air through underground ducts before drawing it through the house; and
- rainwater harvesting for irrigation, toilet flushing, and fountains.

What does "green" mean?

Someone who builds a million dollar house out of straw (yes, that's been done, too!) probably doesn't end up saving either energy or the planet. Houses on that scale inevitably leave a deep imprint. Sustainable architecture, on the other hand, addresses the need for all of us to live and build more lightly on the earth. While primitive housing may leave no permanent impact, "modern" construction does. Hundreds of thousands of houses are built in the United States every year. If only one-tenth of them adopted sustainable techniques, the effect would be noticeable.

Sustainable architecture covers an intertwined set of environmental concerns, some of which may be in conflict. There are few "perfect" materials, so contemporary houses built with sustainable techniques inevitably involve compromise. After all, homeowners, architects, or developers must build according to local codes, as well as make appropriate choices for the local geology, geography, and climate. They must respond to market expectations of comfort and convenience in modern housing, including demands for sophisticated design and architectural intent. Finally, they must balance concerns for safety, durability, and long-term maintenance. These choices are not always easy, but this book offers some ideas on how to make them.

The concept of **sustainable architecture**—choosing materials and techniques that can be maintained for the long-term without exhausting non-renewable resources—applies to four critical areas:

- the choice of materials;
- energy consumed during production of materials, construction, and long-term use (life cycle energy cost);
- minimizing pollution and solid waste generation, again during production, construction, and long-term use;
- the longevity of materials and design to minimize maintenance and replacement costs.

Sustainable materials. Whenever possible, choose materials with recycled content, or made from easily renewable resources. The products themselves should not be hazardous to workers during fabrication or installation, or to people who ultimately live or work in the building.

Casa de Paja uses many recycled materials, from newspaper as ceiling insulation to Expanded Polystyrene Styrofoam® from a supplier who incorporates recycled content. The house uses no lumber from old-growth forests. Compacted earth subflooring replaces an energy-consuming, high-polluting concrete slab; low-temperature-fired Saltillo and Talavera tiles from Mexico substitute for high-temperature-fired ceramic tiles on floors and counters.

Energy efficiency. With only five percent of the world's population, the United States consumes almost 25 percent of its energy resources. Energy consumed in the U.S. has historically drawn on non-renewable sources like oil, on polluting sources like coal, or on potentially dangerous sources like nuclear fission. Renewable, non-polluting energy sources like solar, wind, and geothermal energy are still all too rarely used.

Taking advantage of the sun, the wind, and the earth to reduce long-term heating and cooling costs makes sense for the planet, as well as the pocketbook. Well-insulated houses contribute to these cost and energy savings. Passive solar heating, earth air conditioning, and the high insulation values of straw and cellulose make *Casa de Paja* very energy-efficient.

Energy use also applies to materials: the goal is to select products that consume the minimum amount of energy during production and distribution. Using local products whenever possible reduces energy and transportation costs. Energy efficiency is an implicit concern when looking at homes: does the location contribute to sprawl, or is the community designed to minimize commute times, with reasonable proximity between residential areas, services, and work?

Reduce pollution and greenhouse gases. The less energy burned, the fewer pollutants and greenhouse gases produced, and the less the impact on the ozone layer. Recycle or re-use building materials on site to reduce the amount of solid waste trucked to landfills. Choose finishes rated low for volatile organic compounds (VOCs); products like low-VOC linseed oil or new milk-based paints from Canada not only reduce pollution, but are healthier for people with allergies or multiple chemical sensitivities. Use local building materials to lower the air pollution (and energy consumption) created by moving materials to the site. Avoiding hazardous materials is a given.

Construction waste was recycled at *Casa de Paja*. "Found" materials like pallet strapping were re-used to fasten straw bales over windows and doors. Boiled linseed oil, a comparatively low-VOC product, replaced paint and sealants on floors, walls and ceilings.

Longevity. This critical component of sustainability recognizes the waste of energy, materials, labor, and even capital inherent in rebuilding houses every 50-60 years. Whether for a conventional or sustainable building, the materials used should be durable, easy to maintain, and suited to the location and climate. The structural design and workmanship should ensure long life. The design and materials used in *Casa de Paja* give it the potential to last 200 to 400 years with appropriate maintenance. In the final analysis, perhaps this is its most sustainable characteristic.

What's in the Book?

Mainstreaming Sustainable Architecture is organized by system, rather than chronology of construction. When appropriate, a timeline indicates the implementation of each element during the building process. The selection of sustainable materials is discussed throughout the book.

• Chapter 1. *Sustain the Earth, Sustain the Hearth* considers sustainable architecture throughout history. It shows how techniques can be borrowed from those of builders who constructed wind collectors in the Middle East centuries ago and straw bale houses on the Great Plains during the late 19th and early 20th centuries. The chapter also addresses criteria to consider in evaluating sustainability, These include energy efficiency, air and water pollution, noise control, construction and maintenance costs, and health benefits.

• Chapter 2. *Passive Siting* reviews the overall issues of home design, layout, and positioning a house for passive solar heating. It stresses the importance of latitude, climate, and the specifics of the land in making decisions. This chapter also covers the concept of a house that "learns" with multiple owners over time, using clear spans and other methods to facilitate future remodeling.

• Chapter 3. *Compacted Earth Subflooring* provides significant savings in energy and air pollution compared to a concrete slab. This is the first of the construction chapters, each of which provides a background discussion of the topic, followed by a description of the actual techniques and materials used. This chapter also includes a discussion of radiant heat tubing and Saltillo tile flooring.

• Chapter 4. *Ceiling and Insulation* addresses the structure and materials used for the roof and ceiling, from lumber-efficient trusses to recycled newspaper (cellulose) insulation and ceilings made of bamboo fencing. These environmentally sensitive materials are highly vapor-permeable to facilitate exhausting unwanted moisture and pollutants.

• Chapter 5. *Straw Bale Walls* resolves an oft-stated concern about straw bale buildings: How do you keep water from causing the straw to decay? It describes an innovative approach for venting straw walls to ensure that any moisture can escape to the outside. Detailed photos and illustrations show the relationship between the framing, the bales, and the unique venting system.

• Chapter 6. *Earth Air Conditioning* covers one of the most unusual and successful aspects of *Casa de Paja*— warming or cooling the desert air to 60 to 65°F (winter) or to 72 to 78°F (summer) through a network of 80-foot long underground ducts. Convection currents, stimulated by a tin roof that reaches close to 200°F in the summer, pull the cooler air through the house as hot air escapes through the roof ridge vent. The duct system has already demonstrated significant savings in both heating and cooling costs.

• Chapter 7. *Rainwater Harvesting* for *Casa de Paja* goes beyond the usual use of rainwater for irrigation. It collects rainwater (with back up from the well) through an active system to flush toilets, feed an outdoor fountain, and supply the solar-powered drip irrigation system. Passive rainwater harvesting and distribution occurs through the use of such

landscaping techniques as swales (shallow ditches filled with gravel), earth berms (shallow dams that retain water in a desired location), and ponding (preventing rapid runoff and erosion by holding water until it can seep into the ground).

• Chapter 8. *Xeriscaping* reviews what has become a standard method of desert landscaping—the use of native plants with minimal water needs. It also describes how the choice of plants interacts with the harvesting techniques of the previous chapter to distribute precious water wisely.

• The *Epilog*, an interview with the couple who bought *Casa de Paja*, describes their experiences living in the house, including the elements they have found the most surprising.

• *Appendices* list where the "green" materials used in *Casa de Paja* may be purchased. A glossary and resource list provide additional information.

If you've ever dreamed of owning an environmentally friendly house, or simply of remodeling your current home to reduce the cost of water or energy, this book will stoke your imagination. Whether you read it from cover-to-cover, or access individual chapters as a reference, *Mainstreaming Sustainable Architecture* will be a useful guide to preserving environmental principles, the planet, and your peace of mind.

Mainstreaming Sustainable Architecture

CHAPTER 1

Sustain the Earth, Sustain the Hearth

Sustainable architecture goes far beyond energy conservation, which drew attention in late 1960s and early 70s following a worldwide oil shortage. Sustainability emphasizes the relationship of what architects call "the built environment" (i.e., man-made construction) to local geography, micro-climates, and indigenous materials. At the same time, sustainable design often seeks to incorporate the wisdom of traditional, generally non-professional builders, who constructed what is referred to as **vernacular architecture.**

Human communities have survived in hostile environments from the arid deserts of the Middle East to the icy horizons of the Arctic for thousands of years. Our early ancestors had to use available materials to create shelters and other buildings appropriate to the climate and geography of their region. Millennia of human presence have affected the already changeable elements of climate and geography (e.g., global warming, increasing amounts of desert land), further heightening the challenge of living within the constraints of the natural world.

Updating the lessons learned by early civilizations may not only help us create buildings that are more in harmony with the earth, but may even help heal it. For example, the La Paz Residence Hall at the University of Arizona, Tucson (seen in Figure 1.1), includes a wind catcher derived from the design of an ancient *malqaf* (seen in Figure 1.2). A malqaf consists of a shaft extending high above a building, facing the prevailing wind. It channels any cool breeze into the interior. Windcatchers like these have been found throughout the Middle East and half a world away — on 1200-year-old buildings in Peru, where "sea scoops" caught the ocean breeze.

For centuries, people in India, Egypt, and elsewhere hung wet reed mats over window openings to keep out dust and to cool and humidify the air. (A modern evaporative swamp cooler operates basically the same way.) The La Paz residence hall substitutes cellulose filters with a fine jet spray.

The residence hall also incorporates narrow courtyards, clustered buildings to provide thermal mass, brick screens, and rainwater harvesting, all of which draw on architectural traditions used in regions from the Middle East to Mexico.

Desert cultures were well aware of the value of small openings for ventilation, generally incorporating latticework, louvers or shutters, rather than a few large openings. This approach reduces glare, blocks the sun, distributes airflow, slows wind to drop out airborne dust, and provides privacy.

Traditional builders reduced the hostility of the desert environment by closing outer walls and opening their homes onto an interior courtyard. Protected from the morning sun, a courtyard serves as a reservoir of cool air for most of the day. Breezes refresh inhabitants as cool courtyard air is pulled through the house by convection. Later in the afternoon, the hotter courtyard acts as a chimney, drawing warm air out of the house.

Casa de Paja, as we will see, draws on some of these same traditions.

Figure 1.2 Back view of windcatchers on homes in Tatta, Pakistan. From **Spectacular Vernacular: The Adobe Tradition** *by Jean-Louis Bourgeois and Carollee Pelos, New York, Aperture. © 1978-1996.*

History of the Sustainable Architecture Movement

The first use of "sustainability" in connection with contemporary environmental analysis occurred in *World Conservation Strategy,* a 1980 publication of the International Union for the Conservation of Nature. Interest in vernacular architecture several hundred years old began to flourish a few years later in the then-rapidly growing areas of Saudi Arabia, Egypt, and Yemen, and its precepts were later adapted to industrial buildings in the U. S.

In 1987 the World Commission on Environment and Development, established by the United Nations, defined the principle of sustainability in its publication, *Our Common Future:* "Economic growth can and should be managed so that natural resources are used to ensure the quality of life of future generations." The UN-sponsored Earth Summit held in Rio de Janeiro in 1992 issued *Agenda 21*, laying out the first comprehensive outline for sustainable development, including protection of the global commons (e.g., sea, air, and rain forests).

The definition of architectural sustainability (also called ecological, biological, or "green" building) has since become as varied as the architects, ecologists, developers, and environmentalists who practice it.

Thomas Fisher, in a 1993 editorial in *Progressive Architecture,* described sustainable architecture more specifically as that which "conserves energy, uses renewable or recyclable materials, reduces our dependence on fossil fuels, and attempts to create more intimately scaled buildings and communities."

Bill Mollison elaborated the U.N.'s long-range criteria in his 1994 book *Introduction to Permaculture,* saying "the aim (of sustainable architecture) is to create systems that are ecologically-sound and economically viable, which provide for their own needs, do not exploit or pollute and are therefore sustainable in the long term."

Ten years after *Our Common Future,* James Steele returned to its precepts in his book, *Sustainable Architecture: Principles, Paradigms, and Case Studies*, saying that it "meets the needs of the present without compromising the ability of future generations to meet their own needs."

Most recently, various Green Builder programs around the country have formalized criteria to give developers and architects more specific goals for sustainability, such as:

- avoiding construction in ecologically fragile areas;
- favoring techniques that restore rather than destroy the environment;
- avoiding materials harmful to human and animal health;
- reducing air, water, and solid waste pollution;
- maximizing the use of building materials with recycled content;
- using materials with low-environmental impact during production, construction, and long-term use;
- reducing and recycling construction waste;
- using water-conserving plumbing fixtures;
- incorporating rainwater harvesting or gray water techniques for irrigation;
- controlling noise;
- assessing long-range savings;
- strengthening the local economy.

All these definitions recognize the benefits of sustainable practices: lower maintenance costs, better indoor air quality, and reduced environmental impact. Ultimately, however, the driving force for "green" buildings must come from those who want to inhabit them: without consumer demand, such houses won't be built.

History of Straw Bale Construction

For generations, traditional peoples around the world utilized grass, reeds, straw, and leaves for shelter against the elements. In temperate climate zones, where permanent dwellings are primarily found, shelter also demands good insulation or materials with a large thermal mass to store heat. From the plains of Nebraska (see Figure 1.3a) to the fields of Alabama (see Figure 1.3b) and the steppes of the Ukraine, straw bale buildings met this requirement while drawing on an indigenous building material.

Early homesteaders on the Great Plains recognized that treating bales as oversized bricks was easier than building sod houses, and that the fields of natural prairie grass made bales the fastest form of construction. The invention of steam-powered baling equipment in the late 1800s in the United States, combined with timber-poor reality of the environment, further drove the use of straw and hay bales, particularly around the Sand Hills area of west Nebraska.

Once straw bale houses proved their insulation value in Nebraska's cold winters and hot summers, they were plastered and considered permanent housing. The earliest record of a public building made of straw bales is a one-room schoolhouse built around 1886 in Bayard, Nebraska. Several bale buildings constructed before 1921 are still in use: the headquarters and bunkhouse at the Fawn Lake Ranch near Hyannis, Nebraska, and a home (now used for storage) in

Figure 1.3a Pilgrim Holiness Church, constructed of straw bales in Arthur, Nebraska, 1928. Photograph by Catherine Wanek.

Figure 1.3b Burritt Mansion Museum, Huntsville, Alabama. Photograph by Catherine Wanek.

Fawnville, South Dakota. In the late 1930s straw bale construction peaked, with many houses, churches, and museums of that era still standing and in use.

As mass-produced construction materials became more available and less expensive, bale building slowed in the 1940s-60s. During the early 1970s, when appropriate technologies became a focus of rising ecological awareness, the magazine *Shelter* carried a story about straw bale buildings that renewed interest in the technique. Since then, baled buildings have gone up at an increasingly rapid rate. New Mexico issued its first experimental permit for a non-load bearing straw bale house in 1991, allowing such houses to qualify for insurance and bank loans. Since then, both New Mexico and Arizona have issued an unlimited number of permits; New Mexico published straw bale construction standards in 1995.

Similar interest and growth in straw bale buildings has occurred in Canada, France, Mexico, Central America, Finland, and the Ural Mountains in Russia.

Criteria for Assessing Sustainability

Long-term thinking about sustainable architecture recognizes that higher upfront costs may be offset by future savings in replacement or maintenance costs, and by reducing long-term energy consumption. The concept of **life cycle inventory** (LCI) was developed to tie cost to the concept of sustainability, allowing various products and methods to be compared.

The need for a credible means of validating "green" product claims has led to an internationally recognized standard that assesses the environmental burden of a particular product and its use over time. LCI provides a quantitative rating for environmental inputs (e.g., raw materials, energy consumed in fossil fuels, or electricity) and outputs (e.g., air- and water-borne pollutants, solid or toxic wastes, and the cost of disposal).

Pioneered in the early 1970s by Dr. Ian Boustead at the Open University in Sussex, England, LCI is widely used in Europe. The U.S. Environmental Protection Agency drafted LCI guidelines that have yet to be widely accepted here, however.

In the interim, various programs have established their own sustainable criteria. For instance, the Green Builder Program of the Home Builders Association of Central New Mexico suggests that green architecture address four key areas: energy, materials, waste reduction, and water conservation. Let's look at these four elements of sustainability in greater detail.

Energy efficiency

Roughly half of all energy used worldwide goes into buildings, with two-thirds of that used in homes. Residences consume energy for heating and cooling (70 percent), hot water (20 percent), and lighting and powering appliances (10 percent). A typical single family home uses 50,000 to 70,000 **BTUs** (British Thermal Units) per square foot per year. A "green-built" house can reduce energy use by 75 to 100 percent by:

- using natural energy sources such as solar, wind or geothermal;
- saving energy with well-insulated structures (for every BTU consumed in producing insulation, 12 BTUs are saved each year);
- installing energy-efficient water heaters, appliances, lights, and heating/cooling systems;
- designing to obtain the maximum benefit of both natural and artificial light, such as skylights or task lighting.

Building materials

Many standard building materials require a great deal of energy to produce. They may also reduce the earth's store of non-renewable resources, pollute the air or water, and generate solid waste during extraction and construction.

For instance, processing aluminum requires vast amounts of energy, produces toxic wastes, and consumes huge quantities of fresh water. Although 30 percent of all the aluminum produced in the U.S. is now from recycled scrap, barely 20 percent of aluminum from construction sites is re-used. Yet recycling would save 95 percent of the energy used to produce aluminum from ore.

New home construction consumes 40 percent of all the lumber and plywood used in this country. A typical 1,700-square foot wood frame house requires the equivalent of clear-cutting one-acre of forest! The same house built from straw saves about one-third of that total, or 2,000-2,400 cubic feet of lumber. Plywood is created in a laborious production process that bonds together several thin layers of wood (*veneers*) at right angles. It consumes extensive energy and emits toxic fumes from the glues needed for binding veneers.

Concrete is among the worst culprits for energy consumption. The cement that comprises 10 to 20 percent of concrete is the most energy-intensive component to produce. Including the direct fuel consumed to mine and transport its raw materials (limestone and clay), a ton of cement consumes an estimated six million BTUs in production. Pollutants like carbon dioxide, nitrous oxide and sulfur are generated by burning fossil fuels (coal and natural gas) to heat cement kilns to 2700°F, and through the chemical process of calcining lime.

More than 11 million tons of carbon dioxide were generated during the production of 88 million tons of concrete in the U.S. in 1992. (That amount of concrete would build more than 120 Hoover Dams or pave an eight-lane highway around the equator.)

It took more than 500 trillion BTUs to produce those 88 million tons, equal to 0.6 percent of total U.S. energy use that year. Given that concrete represents only about 0.06 percent of the U.S. gross national product, its production is approximately 10 times as energy-intensive as the overall economy. A new product called autoclaved cellular cement tries to reduce both energy consumption and solid waste by re-using fly ash (the residue from the coal used to fire the kiln) instead of either silica or sands in concrete, or by including fly ash in the cement itself.

To choose sustainable materials, New Mexico's Green Builder program recommends:
- purchasing lumber from ecologically-managed forests;
- selecting materials that require low amounts of energy to get from raw material to delivered product;
- avoiding materials that are toxic to people or the environment;

- selecting products that are engineered to save raw materials;
- choosing products made of recycled and recyclable materials; and
- using durable materials.

Waste reduction

While many cities have now developed programs for curbside recycling or drop-off points, Americans generate an average of 6.2 pounds of waste per person per day. That waste clogs landfills: a ton of recycled paper saves 17 trees and three cubic yards of landfill. Nationally, Americans still throw away enough aluminum every three months to rebuild our entire commercial air fleet. (Figure 1.4 shows a typical landfill.)

Most construction waste also ends up in landfills. It consists primarily of lumber and manufactured wood products (35 percent), dry wall (15 percent) and masonry materials (12 percent). The rest is a mix of roofing materials, metals, plaster, plastics, textiles, glass, and cardboard packaging.

Once again the New Mexico Green Builder program offers suggestions:
- designing for standard-sized materials to reduce waste;
- estimating material quantities accurately;
- choosing products that avoid excessive packaging;
- building a recycling center in a convenient location;
- providing a composting system for organic waste; and
- recycling construction waste.

Water conservation

Water conservation is important everywhere, but particularly in desert areas like New Mexico. (*Casa de Paja* in Corrales receives barely 11 inches of precipitation per year;

Figure 1.4 Bulldozers moving garbage in a landfill. © CORBIS.

anything below 12 inches is considered desert.) New Mexico relies on underground aquifers that are not as large as once thought and that are now replenished more slowly than water is being used.

Americans flush five billion gallons of water down their toilets every day. We could conserve 3.5 billion gallons per day if all toilets met the current code of 1.6 gallons per flush. That would save as much water as flows over all three cascades of Niagara Falls in 90 minutes!

Once again the Green Builder program lays out specific ideas:

- installing plumbing fixtures and appliances that conserve water;
- planting a water efficient landscape (see Figure 1.5);
- using efficient irrigation systems;
- collecting rainwater for irrigation; and
- designing the landscape to prevent water run-off from the property.

Ancient desert cultures have always cherished water, using it in courtyard fountains (see Figure 1.6) as a source of humidity and psychological refreshment. If there was not enough pressure for a fountain, desert homes would substitute earthenware jars filled with water or a *salsabil*, a marble plate tilted against a wall with water trickling over its surface. In the Corrales desert, *Casa de Paja*, too, offers a courtyard fountain.

Casa de Paja: A Demonstration of Sustainability

In the following chapters you'll see how *Casa de Paja* implements sustainable concepts and follows the precepts of a Green Builder program, from reducing the amount of concrete used to incorporating natural finishes. In many ways, such as the underground cooling ducts and courtyard fountain, the house travels the path of the past, drawing on an architectural heritage thousands of years old to create a house that is comfortable today.

CHAPTER 2

Mainstreaming Sustainable Architecture

Sustainable Elements:

Solar Siting and Overall Design

The semi-rural village of Corrales, New Mexico, (population 8,000+) rises on a gradual series of river terraces. An escarpment of blown sand defines the western boundary; wooded river land (the *bosque*) of the Rio Grande, the east. Sitting on the high desert of the Rio Grande plateau at a latitude of 35°15 inches (see map in Figure 2.1) and an elevation of 5,100 feet, the village enjoys a view across the river of the Sandia Mountains blushing watermelon red at sunset (as seen in Figure 2.2). These mountains, at the southern end of the Rockies, climb more than 10,000 feet.

As its Spanish name indicates, Corrales' (corrals) origins lie in ranching and grazing horses. While many residents commute to Albuquerque about 12 miles away or to the high-tech boom town of Rio Rancho immediately to the west, others operate stables, truck farms, or artists' studios.

Much of the soil in Corrales is sandy, the natural vegetation primarily the dusky blue-green of chamisa (rabbit-brush), which flowers yellow in autumn. Since the now-controlled flow of the river irrigates only the bordering riparian habitat, local homeowners often retain native plants with low water demands,

Figure 2.1 Map of the area around Corrales, New Mexico.

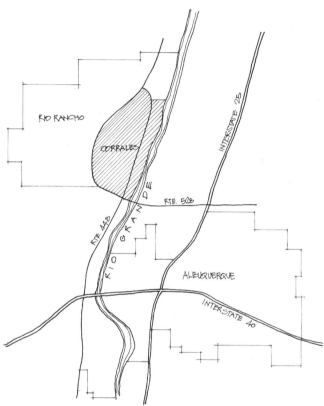

Figure 2.2 Looking east from the site toward the Sandia Mountains.

such as those seen in Figure 2.3. Corrales remains a community in which dozens of cliff swallows nest in arroyo walls (see Figure 2.4), red-tailed hawks swoop down on rabbits hiding in the chamisa, roadrunners scoot across unpaved roads, and cars routinely yield to horses.

In an attempt to maintain this relaxed character, the municipal government zones lots with a minimum of one acre. Perhaps inevitably, the development of Rio Rancho in the 1990s accelerated the transformation of Corrales from an agrarian paradise to an enclave of expensive homes. Although not mandated, new housing has predominantly maintained two pre-existing southwest styles that hug the land, their earth-toned adobe profiles barely visible from a distance.

The first style, *pueblo* adobe seen in Figure 2.5, reflects the architectural precepts of the Pueblo Indians who established earlier villages along the Rio Grande: unadorned thick walls curve softly with

Figure 2.3 Typical native flora in Corrales.

Figure 2.4 Cliff swallows nest in the arroyo walls on the south boundary of the site. The arroyo wall forms the south edge of the drainage easement.

Figure 2.5 A pueblo style adobe house.

Figure 2.6 A territorial style adobe house.

handmade adobe brick and mud wattle; small, deep windows keep out the hot desert sun; and round roof beams (*vigas*) support flat roofs. Narrow peeled saplings (*latillas*) frequently criss-cross the beams to create ceilings.

Following their conquest of the Pueblo tribes in the early 17th century, the Spaniards superimposed details like wrought iron, *portals* (covered porches), detailed wood framing around windows set flat with the exterior walls, square beams, intricately carved corbels, and brick accents. Together, these details denote the second, equally distinctive, *territorial* adobe style seen in Figure 2.6.

Corrales is high desert; temperatures can fall 50 degrees between 10 p.m. and 4 a.m. The desert can mean weeks without rain (Corrales has an average annual precipitation of less than eleven inches), or monsoon rains in summer evenings that turn dry arroyos into crashing rivers. High desert means clean air with visibility that stretches from one horizon to the other with skies that gleam like sapphire. But high desert also means the sun glares like a laser. It means days that bake the earth hard within two hours of a summer sunrise and winter nights that chill vines with hard frost and occasionally dust snow on the desert willows and cottonwoods.

Perched on one of Corrales' river terraces, about two-thirds up the escarpment, *Casa de Paja* (House of Straw) sits on a gently sloping, triangular, one-acre lot (see Figure 2.7) with the broad southern exposure seen in Figure 2.8. It is a perfect location to warm a house with passive solar heating.

Figure 2.6 A territorial style adobe house.

Figure 2.7 Site map showing house location.

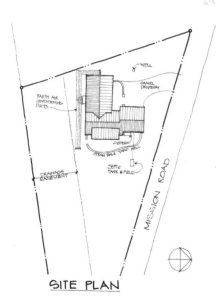

SITE PLAN

Figure 2.8 View from the site to the south.

Passive Solar Design

For all the available sun, high desert climates offer a challenge for solar heating beyond using south-facing windows as a source of solar gain. Heat *loss* from the north and heat *gain* from the east and west must all be minimized. Elevations for all four directions for *Casa de Paja* are seen in Figures 2.9 and 2.10.

Solar siting depends on the particular piece of land, its latitude (which defines the elevation of the sun), and the best angle to the south. While the principles remain the same, solar siting for every house must be adjusted for its location and its rating in degree-days (the average hours of solar exposure in the winter). Fortunately, 90 percent of passive solar potential

NORTH ELEVATION

EAST ELEVATION

Figure 2.9 North and east elevations.

SOUTH ELEVATION

WEST ELEVATION

Figure 2.10 South and west elevations.

Figure 2.11 The angle of the sun changes with the season.

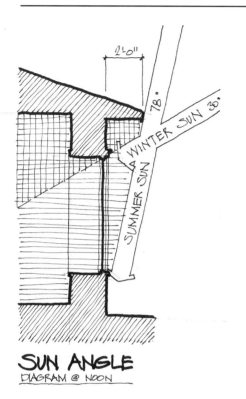

SUN ANGLE
DIAGRAM @ NOON

can be realized as long as a house is sited plus or minus 15 percent of true solar orientation. In most cases, a house can be positioned to conform to the demands of a lot without compromising solar advantage.

Since the sun's elevation changes with the seasons and time of day, a house must be designed to absorb the sun's low rays in the winter, but protect against them in the summer, as seen in Figure 2.11. Pueblo Indians long ago recognized the potential heat gain (and loss) of structural openings. The deeply inset windows of their adobe homes offer cool, dark shelter from summer temperatures topping 90 degrees for days on end; in winter their massive walls radiate heat at night.

Casa de Paja increases solar heat absorption in winter through expansive windows facing south for storage in the floor, as well as in the straw bale walls. Multiple overhangs protect the house, whose territorial windows are not inset, from solar gain in summer. On the south side, an additional 24-inch wide overhang seen in Figure 2.12 shades the Great Room window. The latitude of the house, as seen in Figure 2.8, determines the necessary width of an overhang and its height above the windows.

To offset summer heat gain from the east, an eight-foot wide exterior *portal* (porch), shown in Figure 2.13, shields the

Figure 2.13 A deep portal on the east side of the house minimizes solar gain from that direction.

Figure 2.12 Wide eaves and a secondary overhang above the window of the Great Room shield the south side of the house in the summer.

house. An overhang above the kitchen window, seen in Figure 2.14, also minimizes glare from the low sun of late summer afternoons. In more northern latitudes, heat gain in summer is less of a problem.

Only one bathroom window and three small windows in the garage (see Figure 2.15) face north, reducing exposure to cold winds in winter and limiting heat loss. The enclosed courtyard on the north, shown in Figure 2.16, also helps reduce heat loss in the winter. The large south and east facing windows flood each living space with daylight.

Current costs dictated the decision to omit rooftop solar collectors. Collectors would have added $5,000, or 300 percent above the cost of the windows, but would not have contributed enough extra solar gain to be worth the expense. In colder climates, solar collectors may recoup their investment by reducing the cost of winter heating more significantly. For Corrales' climate and latitude, the benefits simply do not justify the cost. This, of course, may change in the future if the cost of solar cells comes down and individual homes are able to "sell" power back to the electric grid.

Figure 2.14 The entry overhang shields the west-facing kitchen window.

Figure 2.15 Only three small garage windows face north.

Figure 2.16 An enclosed courtyard on the north side of the house helps protects the house from winter wind.

Figure 2.17 Double thermal-paned Pella
low-emissivity windows like these are
used throughout the house.

Thermal Mass and Insulation

Good insulation is critical to effective solar heating (and to earth air conditioning, as we'll see in Chapter 6). Insulation is rated in R-values; the higher the R-value, the better the insulation. Standard stucco houses with fiberglass insulation in the roof and ceiling generally have walls rated around R-19 and roofs around R-30. In contrast, *Casa de Paja's* 18-inch deep straw walls are rated R-40 to R-42 and its cellulose (recycled newspaper)-insulated roof is rated R-55. Straw absorbs and radiates heat slowly, moderating temperature variation.

Even the compacted earth subflooring covered with insulating foam, engineered fill, and Saltillo tile flooring (see Chapter 3) contribute to the passive solar qualities of the house. As we'll discuss in Chapter 6, the entire circulation system of *Casa de Paja*, including the sun-heated tin roof, operates synergistically to move air through the house via convection currents.

Once this house is warm, it stays warm longer; once it is cool, it stays cool longer. Consequently, the house maximizes the efficiency of its heating and cooling systems and will reduce utility-operating costs in future years.

To further improve solar efficiency, all the windows (324 square feet of glazing) are rated from R-2.77 to R-2.94. These double thermal-paned windows seen in Figure 2.17 help limit heat gain in summer, reduce heat loss in winter, and minimize damage from ultraviolet (UV) rays, which can fade furniture and paintings.

Other Design Principles

Designed to blend with neighboring homes, the territorial style of *Casa de Paja* meets contemporary demands for convenience and architectural sophistication. The 2,356-square foot house includes three bedrooms, two full baths, and a Great Room that serves as combination living/dining room/den (see Figure 2.18). An attached garage, designed for potential conversion into a fourth bedroom, home office or den, is reached through the utility/laundry room off the kitchen.

At the west end of the house, the master bedroom, with its own bath and walk-in closet, offers privacy from the demands of family. The Great Room, with its large corner fireplace, is acoustically insulated from the living quarters with cellulose in the wall between the Great Room and the bedroom.

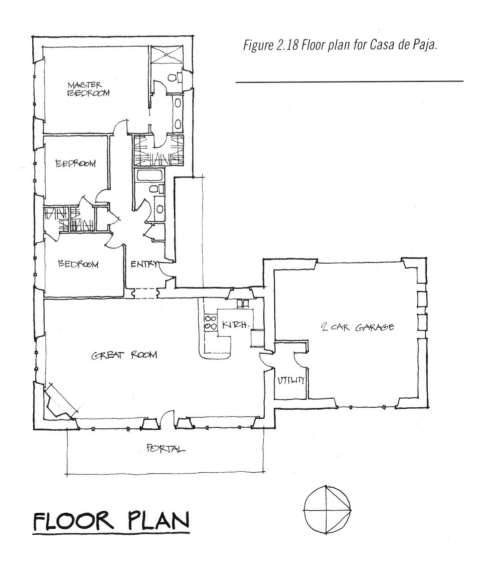

Figure 2.18 Floor plan for Casa de Paja.

FLOOR PLAN

Figure 2.19 Clear span areas are seen in this structural plan sketch. Diagonally hatched areas show the load-bearing wall and locations where concrete was poured (plus the garage slab).

The single-most innovative design element is the way the straw bales are enveloped with air to ensure that they are properly vented. As we'll discuss in greater detail in Chapter 5, this design protects the straw from moisture that can cause the bales to rot, while facilitating the movement of air and encouraging the venting of any harmful chemicals. It is all part of creating a house that "breathes."

Layout: A House That Learns

Casa de Paja "learns" with multiple owners over time, letting them remodel interior spaces easily according to their individual needs. Remodeling is facilitated by large clear-span construction, the minimal use of load-bearing interior walls, and placing interior partition wall framing over the tile.

The house consists of one small space (garage/utility room) and two large open spans — the Great Room/kitchen and the sleeping quarters, as seen in Figure 2.19. The same figure shows that the only true interior load-bearing wall separates the two clear spans from each other. Another load-bearing wall between the kitchen and the garage/utility room uses exterior wall construction and straw bale insulation for thermal mass.

The large clear-span spaces seen in Figure 2.20 make it easy to reconfigure interior walls as needed, whether to combine two bedrooms, to create a hallway access to the master bath, or to utilize existing closet space as a alcove for built-in furniture or shelves.

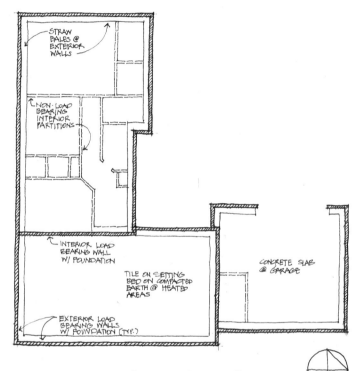

STRUCTURAL PLAN

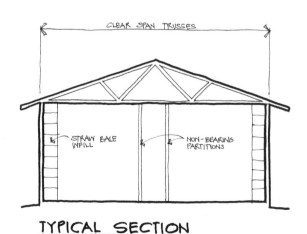

TYPICAL SECTION

Figure 2.20 Cross-section of typical clear span.

Adapting standard office construction techniques to residential construction further facilitates remodeling. With the wood framing for the walls placed *above* the tile floor (see Figure 2.21) and below the ceiling beams, future owners will find it easy to move interior walls. This reverses the standard construction process in which walls are framed first, and floors are laid and ceilings plastered only up to the wall surface.

Bolts secure the bottom plate for the interior wall framing through the tile to the mortar below, as shown in detail in Figure 2.22. Colored wax putty can be used to seal any hole left in a tile if a wall is moved.

The 2x4 truss system seen in Figure 2.23 avoids old style construction techniques that would typically consume multiple 2"x12"x23' beams of old-growth Douglas fir. The trusses use the minimum amount of lumber for maximum structural integrity. As a standard practice, an effort is made to ensure that trusses and framing lumber are cut only from second and third-growth forests.

Figure 2.21 Instead of running only up to the wall surface, the floor tiles in Casa de Paja run beneath the interior wall framing, which is bolted through the tile.

Figure 2.22 Detail of bolting frame through the tile.

Figure 2.23 Truss roof support.

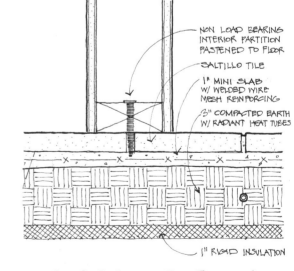

NON LOAD BEARING INTERIOR PARTITION FASTENED TO FLOOR

SALTILLO TILE

1" MINI SLAB W/ WELDED WIRE MESH REINFORCING

3" COMPACTED EARTH W/ RADIANT HEAT TUBES

1" RIGID INSULATION

FLOOR SECTION

Figure 2.24 New Mexico's **Standards for Non-load-bearing Baled Straw Construction**.

The Permitting Process

As in any construction, there is a structured process of permits and building inspections. The state of New Mexico, the County of Bernalillo, and the village of Corrales require the following permits to construct a home; requirements for a straw bale house were no different. Together the permits cost about $1,000.

- Septic tank permit from the state of New Mexico
- Building permit from Corrales
- State of New Mexico building permit
- Separate systems permit and inspections for
  - plumbing
  - electrical
  - low-voltage electrical
  - heating, ventilation and air conditioning
  - well and water supply system
  - natural gas line.

New Mexico is one of the states that has taken the lead in developing standards for straw-bale construction, with an estimated 500 homes already built. Its published standards *(Standards for Non-load-bearing Baled Straw Construction*, State of New Mexico, Regulation & Licensing Department, Construction Industries Division, 1997, shown in Figure 2.24) lay out clear principles for builders, specifying foundation and framing requirements, and delineating standards for fastening bales to the frame. As long as a straw bale house conforms to this code, it is not considered "experimental." Enough straw bale houses have been constructed in New Mexico that there is rarely a problem financing or insuring a straw bale house built to code. This may not be true in all states.

The straw bale code requires that a builder secure the straw bales to the foundation using rebar set into concrete stem walls. It also mandates structural drawings, such as the one in Figure 2.25, stamped by an engineer. By comparison, conventional homes in New Mexico require only unsigned drawings, other than for the roofing truss system, which routinely comes with stamped drawings.

Figure 2.25 A signed structural drawing submitted for approval.

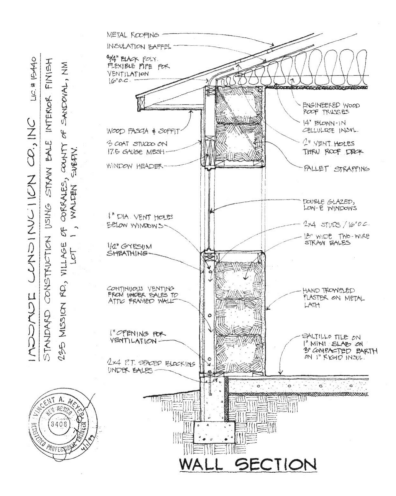

WALL SECTION

The requirement for stamped structural drawings increased the cost of *Casa de Paja* plans by about $1,000 beyond the $3,000 norm. New Mexico doesn't require an architect's signature as long as an engineer has signed for structural integrity. However, a builder in other states might face fees up to 10 percent or more of the cost of the house for an architect's signed drawings.

States may inspect buildings at any time to ensure compliance with construction guidelines. For *Casa de Paja*, these standard inspections occurred with no unusual findings:

- Rebar in foundation
- Framing and rebar placement in straw bale
- Lath (interior & exterior)
- Final inspection followed by issuance of a Certificate of Occupancy.

With this background, we're ready to look at the other elements of sustainable architecture that are integrated into *Casa de Paja*. In each of the following chapters we'll look at the purpose and theory behind each element, and then describe the construction process. Let's start with the compacted earth subflooring and work our way up and out.

CHAPTER 3

Mainstreaming Sustainable Architecture

Sustainable Elements:

Compacted Earth Subflooring and Tile Floors

The Hidden Cost of a Concrete Floor

When conventional builders think "subfloor," they routinely think "concrete slab." A straightforward four-inch slab costs $2.25 to $2.50 per square foot. However, few people realize this convenient slab solution contains a high level of embodied energy. Fewer still recognize that concrete slab construction releases a significant amount of carbon dioxide into the atmosphere, thus contributing to the greenhouse effect.

Think about it. From its very beginning, concrete is energy-intensive to produce. First, there's the diesel fuel that powers the equipment during excavating its raw materials (sand and gravel), and the energy cost of transporting raw materials to the production site. During production, concrete, which uses 12 percent cement by volume to "stick together" the sand and gravel, consumes over 1.7 million **BTUs** (British Thermal Units) just to produce the cement needed for a single cubic yard. Finally, there's the energy consumed during transportation and construction.

Furthermore, for every ton of cement produced, a ton of carbon dioxide (CO_2) is released into the atmosphere during manufacture, when natural gas is burned to heat the cement. It stands to reason that the less concrete that is used to construct a building, the less energy is consumed and the less harmful CO_2 is released into the atmosphere.

Savings from Compacted Earth Subflooring

Using a standard 4-inch concrete slab for entire 2356-square footage of *Casa de Paja* would have consumed more than 23 cubic yards of concrete! Instead, less than six cubic yards were poured for a one-inch mortar bed below the tile flooring. The subfloor beneath this consists of two layers of compacted earth, available on site, sandwiching a layer of rigid insulation.

As a result, *Casa de Paja* saved more than 30 million BTUs in energy and reduced the release of carbon dioxide by more than 8900 pounds! Figure 3.1 compares the embodied energy and carbon dioxide release for the concrete used in *Casa de Paja* as it is

Figure 3.1 A comparison of the subflooring in Casa de Paja versus standard concrete slab construction in terms of embodied energy and carbon dioxide released. Neither column includes the energy costs of transporting materials or preparing the site.

ENERGY SAVINGS WITH SUBFLOOR		
	Standard Construction	Case de Paja
Concrete for floor of 2356 sq. ft. house	4" slab x 1927 sq. ft. = 23.79 cu. yd.	1" mortar bed x 1927 sq. ft = 5.95 cu. yd.
Conversion factor 1.7 million BTUs/yd	23.79 cu. yd. x 1.7 = 40.44 million BTUs	5.95 cu. yd. x 1.7 = 10.11 million BTUs
Case de Paja savings	*30.33 Million BTUs*	

constructed, versus what would have been used with standard construction. The extra labor costs for the compacted earth subfloor, which included research time, were more than made up by the savings in concrete.

Construction: Compacted Earth Subflooring: Part 1

MAY	JUNE	JULY	AUGUST	SEPTEMBER

Compacted earth subflooring is a realistic option in the Rio Grande Valley, where much of the soil consists of a sand base with very small amounts of clay or biological content. The technique can be used in other geological terrain, although it would not work well in the marshy soils of the Southeast or in soil with high clay content. In such areas, dirt must be purchased from a sand and gravel supplier and transported to the site.

After clearing the building site, a small bulldozer excavated the gently sloping site to create a flat pad for the house. The excavated soil was saved for the top layer of engineered fill. As with any construction, plumbing and electrical conduits were placed first, as well as the duct work and room vents for the earth air conditioning seen in Figure 3.2.

A bobcat and a compactor (also called a "jumping jack") ran over the site multiple times, since soil can be compacted only six inches deep at a time. The degree of compaction needed depends on the amount of clay and water in the soil and the gradation in soil particle size. Soil engineering testing labs will analyze a proctor sample to assess the maximum density of the soil and determine the amount of compaction needed. If a lab says that the soil

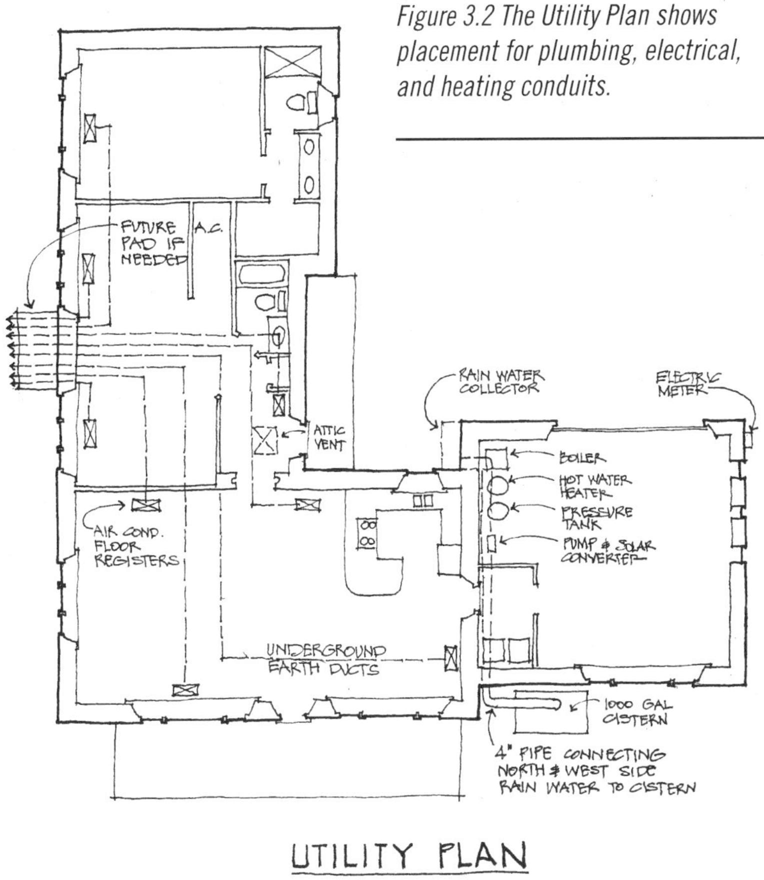

Figure 3.2 The Utility Plan shows placement for plumbing, electrical, and heating conduits.

UTILITY PLAN

does not have enough load-bearing capacity, it is possible to buy soil from a gravel yard. From experience with soils in the Corrales area, the necessary 95 percent compaction and load capacity were reached when the compactor stopped leaving a dent in the earth.

Figure 3.3 The exposed rebar was inserted at least seven inches deep in the stem walls. A straw bale will later be stacked over each piece of rebar.

Construction: Wall Foundations

MAY	JUNE	JULY	AUGUST	SEPTEMBER
■				

A concrete footing was poured for the exterior stem walls, one interior load-bearing wall footing, and a wall footing between the house and the garage. (Figure 2.19 showed where concrete was poured.)

The stem walls were widened to 24 inches on the top so that the straw bales would rest on the same base as the exterior framing. To comply with code requirements, rebar was placed in the exterior stem walls at least seven inches down, as shown in Figure 3.3. A piece of rebar runs through each of the bales in the first course and halfway through the second.

Figure 3.4 Expanded Polystyrene Styrofoam (EPS) R-Guard® panels were placed over compacted earth for insulation purposes.

Construction: Radiant Floor Heating Tubes

MAY	JUNE	JULY	AUGUST	SEPTEMBER
■				

First, one inch Expanded Polystyrene R-Guard® (EPS) panels were placed over the compacted earth. EPS is a standard building product with an insulation factor of R3.85 at 75°F; the supplier of these panels uses recycled material in his product. Figure 3.4 shows these panels, already covered with a wire grid and some radiant heating tubes.

A wire grid of six-inch squares was laid over the EPS foam, both to reinforce the concrete and to help hold the heating tubes in place (see Figure 3.5). Kitec® radiant floor heating tubes were looped above the foam. The garage has radiant heating so it can be converted easily in the future to a fourth bedroom, home office, or den. Figure 3.6 shows a cross-section of the half-inch diameter tubing, which consists of an aluminum tube laminated to interior and exterior layers of plastic.

Figure 3.5 Radiant heating tubes are held in place by a wire grid laid over the EPS foam panels.

Many people place heating tubes directly over dirt, inadvertently contributing to their reputation for poor thermostatic control. Placing R-4 insulating foam under the tubing in *Casa de Paja* increased the efficiency of the heating tubes by forcing the heat upward into the house and will save money on utilities in the future. Installing foam padding and carpet *above* the heating tubes, (as done in most houses) would have created a surface layer of insulation. In effect, the tubes would have warmed the soil below instead of the house above them. As a result of the thermal flywheel effect—the larger the mass, the harder it is to push—it would take forever to warm a house. Using tile instead in *Casa de Paja* makes the radiant heating more responsive to thermostat changes and will keep the house within 2°F of the setting.

To further improve energy management, the radiant tubes were installed in four independently-controlled temperature zones (see the Floor Plan in Figure 2.18):

- the Great Room/kitchen
- the garage/utility room
- the master bedroom and bath
- the two remaining bedrooms and bath.

An energy-efficient natural gas boiler heats the water in the tubing. The system could be converted easily to a solar-powered heating system if energy prices rise to make that alternative cost-effective.

To protect against bugs, mold, mildew, and small animals, natural boron (Neobor®) was sprinkled around the radiant tubing, electrical conduits, air ducts, plumbing pipes, and exterior walls.

Construction: Compacted Earth Subflooring Part 2

A three-inch deep layer of compacted dirt (engineered fill) was replaced over the tube-crossed foam. (See the cross-section in Figure 3.6.) The earth that was saved during excavation was re-compacted with a small bobcat and the "jumping jack," until it appeared as it does in Figure 3.7. Although the earth cushions the radiant heat tubing to prevent damage, the tubing itself was pre-tested by driving a car over it on asphalt to ensure that it could withstand the pressure of the equipment. A standard four-inch concrete slab was poured over the garage floor.

Figure 3.6 Detail sections of a heating tube and flooring layers.

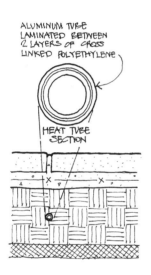

ALUMINUM TUBE LAMINATED BETWEEN 2 LAYERS OF CROSS LINKED POLYETHYLENE

HEAT TUBE SECTION

Figure 3.7 Earth subfloor after compaction.

Mortar Bed and Saltillo Tile

Unlike the sequence in most houses, the tile was laid after exterior framing and the straw bale walls had been erected, but *before* interior framing took place. (See Chapter 5 for details.) This approach, which could be adapted to any house, allows semi-permanent interior walls to be moved easily in the future, letting the house "learn" from its owners. It also means there is no need to rip out flooring or re-lay tile when remodeling occurs.

Saltillo tile is a handmade, low-impact material. Made in Mexico from native clay, Saltillo is an unglazed, soft tile produced through low-temperature firing. Often, Mexican producers of the tile utilize natural or renewable materials, such as straw, wood shavings, cow chips, or plant refuse as fuel for their firings. Much less energy is expended creating Saltillo tile than creating high-temperature, kiln-fired ceramic tiles. Saltillo is also less expensive per square foot for material acquisition. It cost slightly more to install because of the extra-deep mortar bed under the grout joints and the need to seal the top surface.

The natural variation in tile color contributes to the overall handmade feeling of the house. Tile flooring also avoids the problems inherent in wall-to-wall carpeting and padding, which retain dust and may harbor allergens. Unlike petrochemical-based carpets, which often affect those with Multiple Chemical Sensitivities (MCS), tile exudes no harmful fumes. And it lasts much longer than most carpet, which needs replacement every seven years on average. (Area rugs over the tile do not affect heating to the extent that wall-to-wall carpeting would.)

Construction: Mini-slab and Flooring

Workers used the eight-foot long metal screed seen in Figure 3.8 to level the top layer of engineered fill. The dirt was then covered with expanded metal (diamond) mesh, which was held in place with four-inch long cap nails pushed into the dirt (see Figure 3.9). The tile-setters sprinkled boron over the mesh to protect against unwanted intruders from the soil. Throughout the process, they kept wetting down the ground to ensure that the mortar would cure slowly. Figure 3.6 showed a cross-section of the floor construction above the engineered fill.

Usually tile is laid with a thin layer of mortar or thinset over a four-inch concrete slab. In this case, the tile-setters experimented with several techniques for creating a mortar bed thick enough to act as a mini-slab. In the end, they screeded a one-inch mini-slab (see Figure 3.10) reinforced with expanded metal. After it set up hard, they laid the tile over it as usual with thinset. The mortar itself consisted of standard cement, sand, and lime. Based on observations to date, laying the tile over the engineered fill may actually reduce the amount of future cracking. Since concrete continues to shrink, tiles are much more likely to crack over that surface. Past experience with similar floors has shown that this type of floor will easily withstand the expected load of furniture and people once the house is occupied.

Figure 3.8 Workers use a metal screed to level the engineered fill.

Figure 3.9 Mortar will be poured over the mesh grid held in place by cap nails.

Figure 3.10 Preparing the next section of mini-slab for tile. The mini-slab is allowed to dry before tile is placed. Diagonal corners are previously laid tile.

Construction: Laying and Sealing the Tile

MAY	JUNE	JULY	AUGUST	SEPTEMBER
	███			

After the mini-slab dried, tile-setters placed the tile in a diagonal pattern for interest (see Figures 3.11 and 3.12). Since interior framing did not yet divide the floor space (with the exception of the one load-bearing wall), the tile pattern is continuous throughout the house, as seen in Figure 3.13.

The continuous tile also facilitates remodeling, in keeping with the house that "learns."

Figure 3.11 Tile setter at work.

Figure 3.12 Tile is laid in a diagonal pattern for interest.

41

Figure 3.13 The tile flooring forms one continuous surface throughout the house, with interior framing above it, except in the case of the load-bearing walls.

The tile was grouted with cement sand mortar. To prevent damage, the tile was usually covered with pieces of plywood while it set, and then protected with tarps and drop cloths during painting and plastering. After construction and cleaning, one coat of boiled linseed oil was sprayed on as a sealant before grouting (see Figure 3.14), instead of more commonly used polyurethane. Two more coats were applied after grouting.

Linseed oil maintained the builder's commitment to products that contain a low volume of volatile organic compounds (VOC). (See Materials List in the Appendices.) Many toxic sealants with high levels of VOCs contribute to air pollution and to the problems experienced by those with chemical sensitivities.

Because of the time for experimentation and creating a subfloor, the tile-setters' task was 20 to 30 percent more labor intensive than usual, taking about 80 hours longer than typical for a house this size. However, the added labor cost was offset by the savings from the concrete not used and by reducing the work of concrete finishers. In the next chapter, we'll look at framing, roofing, ceiling, and insulation materials.

Figure 3.14 Spraying linseed oil seed over the tile before grouting. Although the linseed oil is not toxic, the worker uses a mask to reduce the odor.

CHAPTER 4

Mainstreaming Sustainable Architecture

Sustainable Elements:

Materials Used in Framing, Ceiling, and Finishes

Why Materials Matter

Using appropriate materials is essential to sustainable architecture. However, the meaning of "appropriate" is a subject for heated debate, not to mention a source of conflict when actually selecting materials.

According to the interpretation, "appropriate materials" may:

- be indigenous to the area of construction to reduce the cost of transportation in both dollars and energy consumption;
- consume minimal energy during production (most builders and homeowners are not aware of the hidden labor and embodied energy costs of many of today's popular materials);
- be energy-efficient when installed and used to lower the cost and consumption of energy during the lifecycle of the house;
- be drawn from renewable resources;
- produce no lasting harm to the flora or fauna of the area from which the materials are obtained or where construction occurs (this includes minimizing loss of habitat, especially for endangered species);
- maximize the use of recycled content;
- be long-lasting and easy to maintain to reduce the need for replacement, which would be energy inefficient;
- not pollute the earth, air, or water during extraction, production, application, or use;
- minimize solid waste at every step in the process;
- be healthy to live with and in.

As you can imagine, there are few "perfect" materials. For any one material, these criteria may conflict. Trade-offs are necessary even in a house like *Casa de Paja*. For instance, the Saltillo tiles described in the previous chapter require more maintenance than high-temperature ceramic tiles. They are more likely to stain, chip, or crack, even though they use much less energy to produce. The tin (galvanized steel) roof uses significant natural resources to produce, but does not need replacing for many more years than standard roofs and contributes to major energy savings for heating and cooling.

Like solar siting, the selection of appropriate materials depends on the geography and climate of the building site. Transportation costs for Saltillo and Talavera tile from Mexico to New Mexico are reasonable; transportation costs to Alaska or Hawaii would not be! Compacted earth subflooring works well in New Mexico, where the soil is well suited to it, but might actually be more energy consuming than a concrete slab if appropriate soils had to be trucked from a distance.

In some cases, one may compromise on a material to obtain a design benefit, and make up for it with the selection of a more sustainable material elsewhere. The best that can be done is to assess the house overall compared to the materials consumed in a more conventional building.

We spoke about concrete, subflooring, and tiles in the last chapter, and we'll discuss straw in detail in the next one. This chapter focuses on the reasons for choosing some of the less obvious materials used in *Casa de Paja*:

- Oriented Strand Board (OSB) instead of plywood;
- cellulose insulation instead of fiberglass;
- matchstick bamboo fencing instead of plaster ceilings; and
- boiled linseed oil as a surface finish instead of paint or polyurethane.

Finally, we'll talk briefly about stylistic details added to the house to make its design appeal comparable to other houses in the area.

Construction: Exterior & Interior Framing

MAY	JUNE	JULY	AUGUST	SEPTEMBER

The initial framing included all exterior walls and the two load-bearing interior walls shown in Figure 4.1. Wall framing followed standard framing practices, with the frame fastened to the concrete foundation walls. No particular changes were

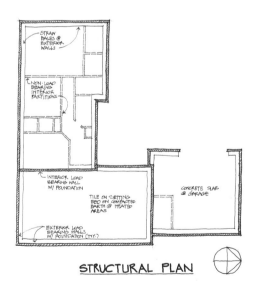

Figure 4.1 Exterior and interior load-bearing walls appear on the Structural Plan.

STRUCTURAL PLAN

Figure 4.2 Standard exterior
framing techniques were used.

made in the framing (seen in Figure 4.2) to accommodate the straw bales described in the next chapter. The exterior walls were covered with gypsum sheeting rather than plywood.

The timing of interior framing was unusual compared to standard construction. As described in the prior chapter, the straw bale walls and tile floor were completed *before* interior framing began. The semi-permanent interior walls were bolted in place over the tile as seen in Figure 4.3 to facilitate future remodeling. (Houses that "learn" were discussed in Chapter 2.)

Many tree farms now produce 2x4s that are guaranteed to come from trees grown expressly for framing purposes. Selecting lumber from a tree farm ensures that the wood will not come from old-growth forests or from stands of trees in habitat critical to endangered species. Certified tree farms also avoid practices like clear-cutting or blocking streams used by spawning fish.

*Figure 4.3 Interior framing was
bolted through the floor tile.*

Construction: Truss & Deck Roofing

MAY	JUNE	JULY	AUGUST	SEPTEMBER

After the exterior walls were framed, the framing contractor assembled the pre-manufactured roof supports, which were composed of trusses made from 2x4s on 24-inch centers (see Figure 4.4). The trusses were covered with Oriented Strand Board (OSB), also known as waferboard. Holes were drilled in the OSB to ensure air access to every curve of the tin roof (see Figure 4.5).

OSB, which has a high content of recycled wood chips, is a more sustainable material than plywood. One of the most common elements in American residential construction, plywood is composed of several thin layers of wood veneers (plies) placed at right angles to each other and bonded together with adhesives.

Plywood is typically manufacturing by converting huge logs into veneers through a series of steps: removing the bark; cutting the log into blocks that will fit the mill's equipment; steaming the blocks to soften the wood fibers; and peeling them into even layers. The layers are then dried, usually by burning natural gas, wood waste, or propane to heat the drying chamber to temperatures around 4000° F. After the dried veneers are graded, they are assembled according to the desired quality and thickness of the final product.

Only interior plywood can use protein-based adhesives, such as soybean or blood glues. Since protein glues are not waterproof, exterior plywood is bonded with phenolic resins, a synthetic (and polluting) product

Figure 4.4 Pre-manufactured roof trusses.

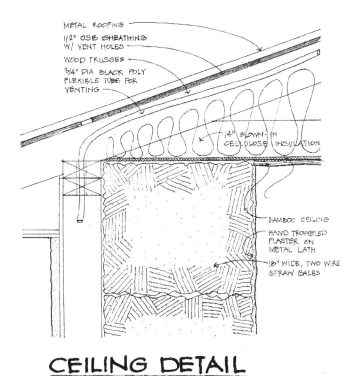

CEILING DETAIL

Figure 4.5 This sketch of the ceiling shows vent holes drilled in the OSB.

produced from formaldehyde and phenol. Once the glue is applied, the veneers are pressed together several times: first in a cold press at low pressure to tack the veneers, and then in a hot press (2300° to 3300°F) at high pressure. The resulting panels are finally cut for size and sanded.

This multi-step process for plywood production requires huge amounts of energy and various polluting glues and chemicals. By comparison, OSB is composed of tree-farmed, fast-growing, small-diameter trees, such as aspen in the Northern U.S. and southern yellow pine in the South. Unlike the high-waste factor for plywood, OSB production at companies like Louisiana Pacific consumes 90 percent of the tree, where the tree bark is burned to heat the drying kilns.

Construction: Ceiling

MAY	JUNE	JULY	AUGUST	SEPTEMBER

The unusual ceiling of *Casa de Paja* was designed to enhance ventilation. The various layers of the ceiling, diagrammed in Figure 4.5, are vapor permeable. They allow vapors and pollutants to escape and permit oxygen to infiltrate, all without losing heat in the winter or cool air in the summer. Allowing the house to "breathe" makes it healthier for everyone, not just those with chemical sensitivities.

Webbing

To hold the cellulose in place, mattress webbing was first stapled to the roof beams (Figure 4.6). This permeable fabric allows vapors and indoor pollutants to escape, but preserves the air circulation pattern. As seen in Figure 4.7, fastening the webbing around the horizontal truss members and to the side edge of the beam at the base of the roof truss reduces bulging. Black webbing might have been less visible through the bamboo than white.

Figure 4.6 Stapling the webbing.

Insulation

The ceiling crawl space is filled with 15 inches of dry-blown cellulose (recycled newspaper) for an insulation value of R-55. Figure 4.8 shows a section of ceiling covered by webbing. It looks almost quilted. To provide acoustic insulation, moistened cellulose was also sprayed between the studs separating all living spaces.

In all cases, the cellulose was treated with boron, which acts as a fire-retardant to yield a Class I fire rating. "Nature's pesticide," boron provides termite protection in dry locations like the walls, ceiling, and below the straw bales. The active ingredient in borax soap, boron has been used as an eyewash and to wash baby's diapers for over 100 years with no harmful effects.

Compare this to fiberglass: manufacturing one square foot of fiberglass insulation one-inch thick consumes over 208 BTUs. Using cellulose instead of 15-inch deep fiberglass to cover the 2300+ square feet of ceiling in the living space saved over 7.3 million BTUs.

Cellulose is also attractive from a value-perspective. It runs only $1.33 per square foot (materials and labor) to insulate walls with a thickness of 5 1/2 inches of cellulose. The 15 inch-deep ceiling insulation ran only $1.17 per square foot. The equivalent R-value in fiberglass batting would cost about twice as much; rigid foam insulation, 5.3 to 9.6 times as much! Some rigid foam still contains chlorofluorocarbons (CFCs) that are harmful to the ozone layer. (The rigid EPS foam used below the subflooring in *Casa de Paja* does not contain any CFCs.)

Frame blocking, illustrated in Figure 4.5, prevented any infiltration of the cellulose insulation into the eaves. Polypipes provided a path for air to flow from the wall cavity behind the straw bales into the closed attic space, and ultimately through the ridge vent in the roof (see Chapter 5).

Figure 4.7 Mattress webbing tacked to roof beams before insulation is installed.

Figure 4.8 A section of ceiling covered by webbing after insulation was blown in.

Figure 4.9. Matchstick bamboo
fencing is used for the ceilings.

Bamboo and Beams

Rolls of matchstick bamboo reed fencing were stapled over the mattress webbing (Figure 4.9). Like the webbing, the bamboo is vapor permeable. Between the webbing and the bamboo reeds, the ceiling is 20 times more vapor permeable than the walls. The fencing echoes (in miniature) the look of traditional *latilla* ceilings common in adobe construction. Bamboo, however, is an easily grown plant that reproduces far more quickly than the tree saplings used for *latillas*.

The decorative, non-structural, hand-adzed beams seen beneath the bamboo reeds were cut from standing deadwood. No old-growth lumber is used anywhere in *Casa de Paja*. As was done with the Saltillo tile and Structolite walls, the bamboo reed ceilings and beams were sprayed with a coat of boiled linseed oil. More coats of oil would result in darker, shinier surfaces. Up to four coats can be applied to satisfy those wishing to duplicate the higher-gloss, lower-maintenance look of polyurethane finishes.

Linseed oil, which dries hard in about one week, needs only an annual surface vacuuming to keep it free of dust. Since linseed oil contains a much smaller quantity of volatile organic compounds (VOCs) than paint or polyurethane, it is also healthier to live in. Most homeowners don't realize that indoor air pollution—whether due to smoke, cooking, lack of ventilation, or chemicals that "out-gas" from building materials — can be two to five times higher than outdoor pollution.

Among many steps to reduce indoor pollution, the American Lung Association recommends such practices followed in *Casa de Paja* as using:

- smooth surfaced flooring instead of carpets;
- non-toxic adhesives to install tile and other materials;
- gypsum board, plaster, or real wood in construction;
- low VOC-emitting paints and finishes, rather than paints that will out-gas for months after application.

Style Details

In keeping with other homes in the area, *Casa de Paja* has a corner fireplace in the Great Room, as seen in Figure 4.10. The fireplace has a hand-carved surround of Cantera (a naturally occurring limestone) and Travertine cut stone. Materials like these are needed in such a high-temperature area.

The exterior trim around the metal-clad Pella windows, which is typical of territorial style houses (Figure 4.11), is also echoed around interior doors (Figure 4.12). These particular windows contain 95 percent recycled aluminum and 50 percent recycled glass. Even their packaging consisted of 30 percent recycled paper, with the remainder created from tree-farmed pulp.

Using recycled aluminum is important. This metal is a finite resource, now extracted by strip mining in predominantly poor, third world countries. Processed in an energy-intensive smelter, aluminum production yields a number of toxic wastes. Scrap aluminum can be recycled to save 80 percent of the energy consumed during production, but recycling is far more common in the West than other parts of the world.

Figure 4.10 Great Room corner fireplace.

Figure 4.12 Territorial style trim on interior doors.

Figure 4.11 Exterior territorial style window trim.

Figure 4.13a Red brick and wood detailing on the east portal add additional territorial details.

The red brick and wood detailing typical of territorial buildings is also found on the patio and ceiling of the east portal (Figures 4.13a and b) and in the courtyard on the north (Figure 4.14). Additional details, such as Mexican-style tin light fixtures in the Great Room (Figure 4.15) and punched tin mirrors in the bathrooms add to the traditional feeling of the house.

Finally, the "truth window" near the front door, shown in Figure 4.16, proves that the walls of *Casa de Paja* are indeed made of straw. In the next chapter we'll see just how those walls were built.

Figure 4.13b. Composite (four 2x6s) structural beam on portal. 2x6s can be cut from tree farm lumber.

Figure 4.14 Brick walkway in the north courtyard continues the detailing.

Figure 4.16 A "Truth Window" located in the hallway proves that Casa de Paja is indeed built of straw.

Figure 4.15 Mexican-style tin light fixture in the Great Room.

Mainstreaming Sustainable Architecture

Sustainable Element:

Straw Bale Walls

Figure 5.1 Venting diagram shows how air moves through Casa de Paja.

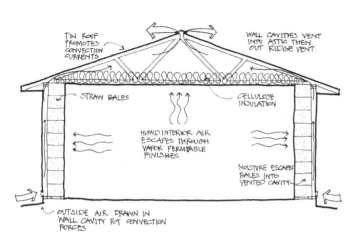

VENTING DIAGRAM

Overcoming Concerns

The wolf who told the three pigs he would huff, puff and blow down their (straw) house must have been thinking about straw walls that rotted from too much moisture. If water enters the wall around windows and doors or from a leaky roof and cannot evaporate, the straw within the walls will eventually decompose, leaving a hollow stucco shell. For that reason, and because straw bales would compress under the weight of a roof, New Mexico building code precludes using straw bales alone in load-bearing walls.

In an ordinary straw bale house, moisture in the bales can move only toward the inside of the house. But that's difficult: the inside of a house is more humid than the outside due to water vapor from showers, cooking, and breathing. Commonly used latex paint impedes airflow and allows moisture to remain in the bales longer than it should. *Casa de Paja* conquers its wet enemy with special venting to the outside that allows moisture to escape from beneath the bottom course and from the outer sides of the stacked straw bales, as seen in Figure 5.1. Thanks to the Second Law of Thermodynamics, moisture in the bales naturally seeks the dryer outside air. This is *Casa de Paja's* secret for longevity. Its innovative approach to venting could allow the house to survive for up to several hundred years—the ultimate measure of sustainability!

The diagram of the wall section in Figure 5.2 shows how bales are placed on 2 x4-inch shims, so their bases rest one and one-half inches above the floor with a vent space beneath them. They are stacked against the interior surface of the studs, not between them, leaving an open-air compartment between the bale surface and the exterior sheeting.

Mini-soffit vents (shown in Figure 5.3) are installed on every vent hole in the studs through the exterior wall to vent the outer face of the straw bales. Vent holes drilled into all the exterior shell framing cavities, as well as through the base plate and top plate, offer air a path to the roof ridge vent. To keep the bale ventilation channel clear to the ridge vent, 3/4-inch polypipe was inserted into the vent holes in the top plate and extended above the cellulose insulation into the attic cavity. Wood blocks prevent air from passing from the eaves into the attic cavity, which would short-circuit the venting pressure. Unlike a conventional home, no vents are placed in the soffit.

The inner walls are unpainted, vapor-permeable, gypsum plaster. Painting the plaster with latex or other paints would have inhibited the transpiration of moisture and contributed to pollution from VOCs.

Figure 5.2 The wall section diagram shows how bales are placed above the shims and inside the surface of the studs. The roof load is already on the exterior walls when the bales are placed. The bales themselves are not load-bearing.

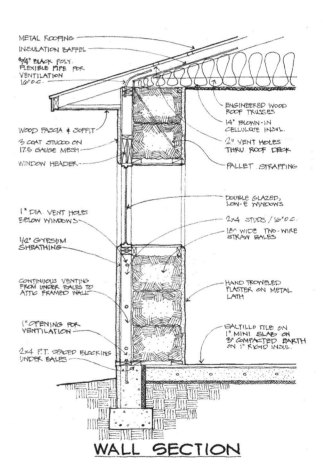

WALL SECTION

METAL ROOFING
INSULATION BAFFEL
3/4" BLACK POLY. FLEXIBLE PIPE FOR VENTILATION 16" O.C.
WOOD FASCIA & SOFFIT
3 COAT STUCCO ON 17.5 GAUGE MESH
WINDOW HEADER
1" DIA. VENT HOLES BELOW WINDOWS
1/2" GYPSUM SHEATHING
CONTINUOUS VENTING FROM UNDER BALES TO ATTIC FRAMED WALL
1" OPENING FOR VENTILATION
2X4 P.T. SPACED BLOCKING UNDER BALES

ENGINEERED WOOD ROOF TRUSSES
14" BLOWN-IN CELLULOSE INSUL.
2" VENT HOLES THRU ROOF DECK
PALLET STRAPPING
DOUBLE GLAZED, LOW-E WINDOWS
2X4 STUDS / 16" O.C.
18" WIDE TWO-WIRE STRAW BALES
HAND TROWELED PLASTER ON METAL LATH
SALTILLO TILE ON 1" MINI SLAB ON 3" COMPACTED EARTH ON 1" RIGID INSUL.

Figure 5.3 Mini-soffit vents with screen backing circle the house.

Figure 5.4 The Martin-Monhart house built of straw bales in Arthur, Nebraska, 1925. It is now open to the public as a family museum. Photograph by Catherine Wanek.

Figure 5.5 Exterior courtyard wall under construction on the east side of the house.

Of course, *Casa de Paja* uses waterproofing under the base shims, below the windowsills, and beneath the exterior stucco to prevent water from getting in. The overall approach tries to reproduce the conditions that have kept some straw bale houses (Figure 5.4) standing on the Great Plains for more than 75 years.

The exterior courtyard walls are built quite differently. For these walls, seen in Figures 5.5 and 5.6, the straw was simply used as a mold for the stucco and will not weaken the wall if it decays. The plaster itself extends eight inches into the ground.

Energy Savings from Straw Bale Walls

A conventional 2x6-inch framed home with five and one-half inches of cellulose insulation is rated about R-22. Straw bale walls like those used in *Casa de Paja* (two-string bales laid flat on their 18-inch sides) have been rated from R40 to R42, depending on the type of straw. The higher the R-value is, the better the insulation. With better insulation, a smaller heating and cooling system can be installed, thus offsetting other construction costs. And the better the insulation, the less energy must be consumed for heating and cooling in the future. The energy-efficiency of straw insulation also increases the likely success of the earth air conditioning system as described in detail in the next chapter.

There are also substantial energy savings from using straw instead of fiberglass as wall insulation. It takes 61 kilowatt hours (3413 BTUs) to produce 1000 square feet of fiberglass one inch thick. *Casa de Paja* has more than 2300 square feet of exterior walls after subtracting glazing area. Using five and one-half inches of fiberglass in the walls instead of straw would have expended more than 771 kilowatt hours or 2.6 million BTUs in energy! Moving up to seven inches of fiberglass to achieve R-22 would have expended more than 3.4 million BTUs.

The United States alone produces about 200 million tons of waste straw per year. Straw that is allowed to decompose slowly through bacterial action produces methane gas; straw that is burned releases carbon monoxide. Both gases contribute to the greenhouse effect. Depending on the type of straw, burning straw releases about five percent of its weight as carbon monoxide. In other words, burning 100,000 tons of straw would release 5,000 tons of carbon monoxide. *Casa de Paja* used 800 bales weighing 50 pounds each. Reusing this straw waste as a building material avoided the release of about one ton of carbon monoxide. Burning straw also generates particulate pollution that irritates lungs and may be carcinogenic.

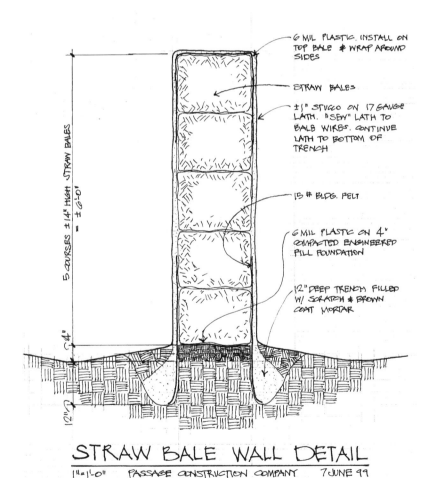

Figure 5.6 Detail of straw bale courtyard wall.

MAY	JUNE		JULY	AUGUST	SEPTEMBER
		████			

Bale composition

The stems of grain left in the field after harvesting are straw. Since cut straw is too long to be tilled into the soil, it is either baled, used as animal bedding, composted, or burned. Oats, wheat, rice, rye, or flax are most often used for straw bale construction, based on what is available locally.

Casa de Paja straw (Figure 5.7) was purchased from a local feed store. It was baled for structural use, which requires more compaction and stronger wire than ordinary baling. According to New Mexico code, structural bales must be sufficiently compressed to remain intact when carried 20 feet while held by one wire. The code also specifies a maximum moisture content of 20 percent.

The straw was delivered shortly before use. Since almost all the straw construction occurred during a dry month, it was possible to leave the straw outside the house. Leftover straw was later stored in the garage. Moisture in the bales continued to dry outside, as well as inside the house during the six-week gap between the placement of the bales and interior plastering. The venting system will ensure that the bales would dry out even if they were damp when installed.

Figure 5.7 These bales of straw meet structural requirements.

The two-wire bales measured approximately 16 inches high (on edge) x 18 inches wide (flat side) and 33 to 39 inches long. Although the original house dimensions were designed to be multiples of bale size, this proved not to be critical. The bales were easy to trim and small spaces were stuffed loosely with straw. One load of straw—slightly over 800 bales—was enough for the house and the freestanding walls around both courtyards.

Construction: Exterior (Shell) Framing and Preparation

MAY	JUNE	JULY	AUGUST	SEPTEMBER

A vapor barrier consisting of two layers of 30 lb. roofing felt paper was placed over the stem wall before framing. Shell framing was standard, with 2x4 inch posts on 16-inch centers, as seen in Figure 5.8. In addition to the base plate, the framers placed two parallel 2x4s with their outer edges 18 inches apart as floor shims (see Figure 5.9) to create a platform so the bales would be raised one and one-half inches from the stem wall. This is one way that moisture dries from below the straw bales. On the outside, the framing was covered with gypsum sheathing and standard stucco, as shown in Figure 5.10.

Figure 5.8 Standard framing used for straw bale construction.

Figure 5.9 Floor shims keep the first course of bales from touching the stem wall, leaving a venting space to the wall cavity.

Figure 5.10 Gypsum sheeting with an outer vapor barrier also provides exterior lateral bracing.

The framers drilled one-inch holes through the floor shims, base plate and top plate into each frame cavity (see Figure 5.11). A small piece of PVC pipe was temporarily placed through each horizontal hole in the base plate, as shown in Figure 5.12, to keep the mini-vents from being filled or covered during exterior finishing. Flexible plastic tubing, seen in Figure 5.13, was permanently placed in the vents of the top plate to prevent accidental closure when cellulose was sprayed into the attic. One lesson learned: In the future, it would be helpful to use similar tubing through the vertical holes in the base plate to prevent straw from possibly clogging those holes.

As a final step in preparation, boron (Neobor®) was sprinkled between the shims to protect against bugs (Figure 5.14). A natural pesticide, boron also acts as a natural

Figure 5.11 Close-up of holes drilled both vertically and horizontally through the base plate to ventilate the straw bale wall.

Figure 5.12 During construction, these PVC tubes kept the vents in the base plate from being covered. At the end of construction, they were replaced with the mini-soffit vents shown in Figure 5.3.

Figure 5.13 Flexible black plastic tubing keeps the vents in the top plate open even after ceiling insulation is installed.

fire retardant and fungicide. Contrary to expectation, straw actually exhibits very little mold or allergy potential as long as it remains dry. There is no more problem with rodents in a straw bale house than with conventional construction as long as the house is sealed, as this one is, to prevent rodents from gaining entry.

Before stacking the bales, a standard building inspection confirmed that the framing was anchored to the foundation, that corners were properly fastened, and that rebar pins were on center for the first course of straw. According to Philip Mann, the inspector from the state Construction Industries Division, "What's done here is far and above code."

Figure 5.14 Boron, a natural pesticide, fungicide and fire retardant, was sprinkled between the floor shims, as well as around pipes running through the compacted earth subflooring, and under the mortar bed for the tile.

Construction: Placing the Bales

MAY	JUNE	JULY	AUGUST	SEPTEMBER
		■		

The framers carried the bales easily by the two wires and set them in place on the flat (18-inch) side, as shown in Figures 5.15 and 5.16. Each bale was secured to the floor assembly by two exposed #4 rebar pins. The initial pieces of rebar had been embedded at least seven inches into the floor assembly and extended halfway through the second course of bales.

Figure 5.15 Carrying a bale.

Additional rows of bales were stacked in running bond, as illustrated in Figure 5.17. Each row was pinned with a three and one-half foot long #4 rebar rod that extended, per code, through a course of bales, and at least halfway up the course above and halfway down the course below. The pins must be placed nine inches from bale ends and centered on the width. Corner bales were also pinned with rebar. Figures 5.18 and 5.19 show a wall under construction and a finished wall.

To fit into small spaces or corners, bales were trimmed with a 3/8 inch steel baling needle, as seen in the series Figure 5.20, and retied with rebar tie wire.

Figure 5.16 Stacking the first course of bales.

Figure 5.17 Diagram shows how bales were set in running bond and pinned with rebar.

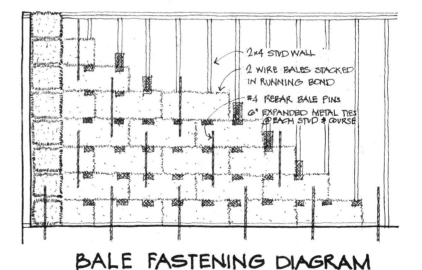

2×4 STUD WALL
2 WIRE BALES STACKED IN RUNNING BOND
#4 REBAR BALE PINS
6" EXPANDED METAL TIES @ EACH STUD & COURSE

BALE FASTENING DIAGRAM

Spaces less than four inches high were easily filled using loose straw (see Figure 5.21). This approach was used to fill gaps between the top course and the roof trusses, as well as over windows. Bales were placed against the load-bearing wall between the kitchen and utility room for acoustic as well as thermal insulation.

When the bales were stacked about four high, the framers vacuumed out the cavity between the bales and exterior wall to keep loose straw from blocking the vent holes.

Figure 5.18 Straw bale walls under construction.

Figure 5.19 Completed straw bale walls.

Figure 5.20 Cutting a bale with a baling needle. First, the framer inserts the baling needle (a). Then he pushes it down (b). Finally, the framer can pull the baling needle through (c).

Figure 5.21 Loose straw was stuffed into small openings around doors and windows and below the roof trusses.

Construction: Fastening the Bales

MAY	JUNE	JULY	AUGUST	SEPTEMBER
	■			

As the bales were placed, the framers nailed every course to the wall studs with flexible metal lathing at each horizontal joint. Every bale was fastened to at least one stud. The lath extends five inches over the edge of each bale as seen in the illustration in Figure 5.22 and the photograph in Figure 5.23. Making the bales an integral part of the framing this way is a totally new method of straw bale construction.

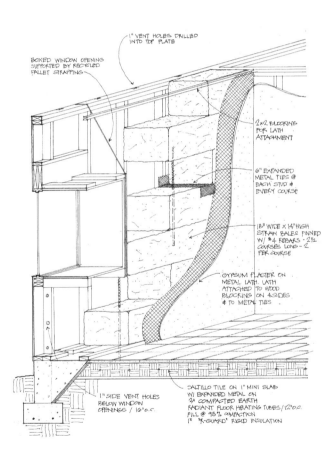

Figure 5.22 The diagram shows how lathing ties each bale structurally to the framing. Note the use of the header over the window to support upper bales.

Figure 5.23 Lathing attaches bales to studs.

MAY	JUNE	JULY	AUGUST	SEPTEMBER
		■		

Figure 5.24 Structural support for the window seats.

For solar purposes, the windows were hung on the outside edge of the window seats, which were designed to be one-bale deep and one-bale high. Small structural beams under the window seats, seen in Figure 5.24, make them stable even without the straw bales. A 2x4 inch box header over each window or door supports the straw bales above it (see Figure 5.25). Recycled pallet strapping fastened to the wall top plate holds the bales in place and supports the header. Since the space above the top course was less than the height of a bale, loose straw was stuffed to fill the gap to the roof truss. The interior of each window and door box was later fitted with plywood, painted, and detailed as seen in the finished window in Figure 5.26.

Once the bales were placed, *Casa de Paja* acquired a sense of mass, providing both sound and temperature insulation that made the house comfortable to work in throughout the summer heat. As we'll see in the Epilog, the sense of mass arising from the ancient idea of thick walls gave the homebuyers an instant sense of comfort and security, particularly in contrast to a contemporary "thin wall" approach.

Figure 5.26 Finished window trim.

Figure 5.25 Recycled pallet strapping supports the header and bales.

Construction: Electrical and Plumbing Conduits

MAY	JUNE	JULY	AUGUST	SEPTEMBER

To ensure that they would fit behind the eventual wall surface, plumbing and electrical conduits were pre-set in the floor assembly to sit behind the face of the bales. The framers hollowed out enough straw to accommodate the conduits and pipes already in place (see Figure 5.27). During rough-in, the plumber pulled out more straw to make space for the pipes and pushed them through the bales.

The electrician hammered a board between bales to make enough space to pull conduit and to stabilize electric boxes. He hollowed out space for electrical boxes also (see Figure 5.28). The wiring, which is UF-cable (underground rated), runs two inches from the face of a wall.

Figure 5.27 Plumbing pipes appear on the face of a bale.

Figure 5.28 The electrician forced spaces between the bales for wiring and pulled out straw to carve room for electrical boxes.

MAY	JUNE	JULY	AUGUST	SEPTEMBER
			■	

Figure 5.29 Sprayed wet cellulose is brushed flat between studs in the Great Room wall.

For soundproofing, wet cellulose (recycled newspaper) insulation was sprayed between the stud walls that divide the living spaces. The wet cellulose was then brushed flat as seen in Figure 5.29.

Metal lathing (chicken wire) for the interior plaster was fastened to the roof nailing strip and floor shims, as seen in Figure 5.30. To maintain the breathability of the interior side of the straw bale walls, two types of vapor permeable gypsum plaster were used. Red Top®, which was used for several layers of base coat, contains wood fiber. Structolite®, which contains no fiber, served as the finish coat. Figure 5.31 shows one of several layers of base coat being applied to the wall surface.

Rather than using a cement dye or wash, the walls were left in the natural variegated tan color of the Structolite®, and sprayed with two coats of boiled linseed oil that was then wiped down. Additional coats of oil can be applied to make the walls more stain-resistant. Unlike latex paint, the oil is a low VOC, vapor-permeable product.

In the kitchen, framing and sheetrock were placed in front of the straw bales on the exterior wall and on the wall bordering the utility room (see Figure 5.32). This made it easy to attach cabinets to the studs, and to install kitchen fixtures, electrical outlets, and plumbing. It also provided an appropriate surface for setting Talavera tile, another low-temperature fired tile, as a backsplash. Talavera tile, shown in Figure 5.33, was also used in both bathrooms.

Figure 5.30 Chicken wire lathing covers the straw to provide a base for the interior gypsum plaster.

Figure 5.31 Mason applying a layer of base coat over the wall.

Figure 5.32 Framing and sheetrock were attached to bales in the kitchen.

Figure 5.33 Talavera tile was used for the kitchen backsplash and counters, as well as in the baths.

Construction: Finishing Exterior Walls

MAY	JUNE	JULY	AUGUST	SEPTEMBER
			███████	

The exterior finish was standard stucco. It consisted of affixing chicken wire lathing and building paper, as shown in Figure 5.34, and applying scratch and brown coats of mortar (Figure 5.35), with stucco for the color coat.

In the next chapters, we'll look at additional elements of sustainable architecture, from earth air conditioning to rainwater harvesting and xeriscaping.

Figure 5.34 Applying exterior chicken wire lathing.

Figure 5.35 Applying the brown coat to the exterior.

CHAPTER 6

Mainstreaming Sustainable Architecture

Sustainable Elements:

Earth Air Conditioning and Tin Roof

Long before the discovery of electricity, Middle Eastern civilizations figured out how to survive the heat of equatorial deserts, where high temperatures average 113°F. The many rich and varied urban civilizations that flourished in Mesopotamia, Egypt, and Israel beginning around 6000 B.C.E found solutions that were energy efficient, renewable, and in tune with the earth.

The accomplished architects and engineers of early Middle Eastern desert cultures devised methods for directing breezes into their homes that are still used today (Figure 6.1) and constructed "chimneys" (minarets) that allow hot air to rise and escape (Figure 6.2). They were the first to develop underground cooling ducts to bring cool air into their homes, temples, and other buildings. Adjusting their architecture to the *pas de deux* of earth and sun, these populations also left behind a rich legacy of art and the foundation of modern mathematics.

Alas, while we still enjoy their art and employ their math every time we write Arabic numerals, we seem to have lost touch with their environmentally attuned architectural secrets. Modern cooling systems fight nature with refrigerated chemical coolants and electrically powered fans and air conditioners. Instead of acknowledging the power of the sun, we often seem to defy it. We dare our buildings to overheat by constructing them in full sun, ignoring the need for awnings, shade trees, and appropriate siting. Our summer utility bills climb ever higher to maintain a comfortable working temperature of 72°-78°F, consuming energy and polluting the atmosphere along the way.

Figure 6.1 This house in Tatta, Pakistan, has a windcatcher 28 feet long. The wind room below it, seen here, has four windows and two doors to regulate incoming breezes. From **Spectacular Vernacular: The Adobe Tradition** *by Jean-Louis Bourgeois and Carollee Pelos, New York, Aperture. © 1978-1996.*

Casa de Paja is earth-aware. Its systems work together to protect the building from heat and use as little energy as possible for cooling. We've already spoken of how the building materials and design help maintain a stable temperature:

- straw bales and cellulose are excellent insulators
- deep portals and overhangs shade the house from the worst of the sun;
- windows with high-R values and low emissivity are used throughout;
- the house was designed to minimize the number of windows on the north and west; and
- *Casa de Paja* was sited to take advantage of passive solar heating.

These features alone reduce the amount of cooling that will be needed. Beyond that, *Casa de Paja* strikes out into innovative territory: it takes advantage of the stable temperature of the earth to cool hot desert air to 69°- 78°F in summer and warm it to 65°F in winter. The warmer temperature of the tin roof, which can reach 210°F in the summer (almost enough to boil water) yields a passive **convection current** updraft. The convection current draws exterior air into the underground ducts and then through the house, replacing the air drawn up through the central air vent and ceilings to the roof ridge vent. A power blower was also installed in the central air vent to assist the convection currents in the summer (see Figure 6.3).

Figure 6.2 Minaret (cooling tower). © Corel.

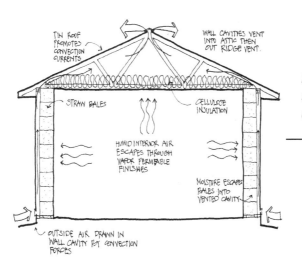

VENTING DIAGRAM

Figure 6.3 Air circulation diagram shows how the tin roof helps generate convection currents.

As the warmer air escapes, fresh air is drawn into the underground ducts and the process begins again. Why does this happen? The space directly below the tin roof of *Casa de Paja* contains the hottest air in the house—and the lowest pressure. The incoming air at the floor is drawn toward the roof, and ultimately out through the roof ridge vent. A temperature (or pressure) gradient is needed, since the air travels more than 150 feet from its source at the air inlets to its exit at the roof!

Air Flow in *Casa de Paja*: Synergy by Design

Each room has an independent intake air duct from outside (Figure 6.4). Although there are no other special air ducts inside, incoming air has several ways to move toward the roof. First, a master attic vent in the central hallway controls the flow of air from the house to the attic cavity. It can be completely or partially closed to retain warm air in winter or to reduce the rate at which air exits, thereby affecting the rate at which new air enters.

Figure 6.4 The Utility Plan shows the location of air ducts and registers.

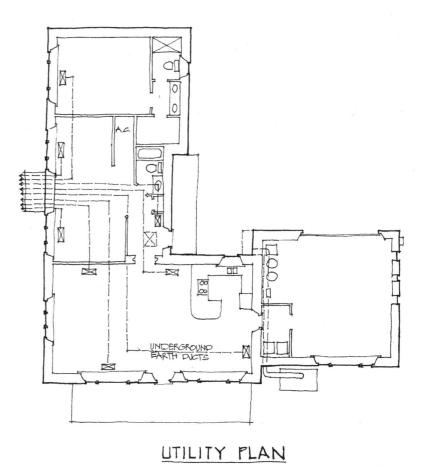

UTILITY PLAN

Air exchange in the house (the rate at which fresh air replaces existing air) exceeds the national standard of 1.5 times every hour of the day. As an added benefit, air exchange facilitates the escape of indoor pollutants, smoke, odors, and water vapor.

Construction: Air Ducts and Inlets

MAY	JUNE	JULY	AUGUST	SEPTEMBER
		■		

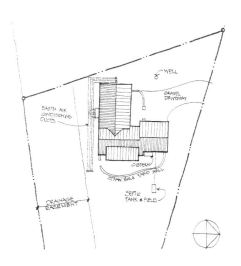

Figure 6.5 Diagram of exterior duct placement.

The air arrives through standard eight-inch diameter metal ducts that extend an average of 80 feet underground (Figure 6.5). The ducts were buried six feet below ground level outside the house; at that depth the constant temperature of the ground is 65°F in winter and 69°F in summer.

Since the air duct temperature has proved to be relatively consistent during a season, both heating and cooling costs are minimized. In essence, heat that has been stored in the ground all summer slowly radiates in the winter, warming the air in the ducts. In the summer, the reverse occurs: warm air in the ducts gradually radiates heat to the surrounding earth, cooling the air before it reaches the house.

By closing the master vent or the floor vents, the rate of airflow can be reduced, allowing the exterior air more time to stabilize at the temperature of the ground. A thermometer measures ambient air temperature at an air inlet, at one of the floor vents, and five feet above the floor (room temperature). As Figures 6.6 and 6.7 on the following page show, the moderating effect of the ducts is quite stunning, especially in winter, with air temperature warming as much as 38°F. During the summer, cooler air from the underground ducts cooled the house throughout the day and into the late afternoon when these measurements were taken. By evening, the heat of the day made its way through the massive straw bale walls. However, convection currents in the house continue through the night, pulling in cool night air, which in turn draws heat from the ground surrounding the ducts. This creates a temperature "lag"

February 2000

February	AM Outside temp	AM Duct temp	AM Indoor temp
1	32	62	66
2	24	62	64
3	28	61	66
4	29	60	64
5	28	60	63
6	32	62	66
7	31	61	64
8	28	62	64
9	46	64	65
10	43	64	65
11	28	61	64
12	26	60	63
13	31	62	63
14	40	60	65
15	42	62	66
16	36	62	65
17	45	64	68
18	34	62	64
19	36	60	64
20	38	61	64
21	42	62	64
22	38	62	64
23	24	62	64
24	42	64	65
25	26	64	66
26	28	64	65
27	32	64	66
28	34	62	64
29	35	63	65

Figure 6.6 February 2000 morning temperature comparison in Fahrenheit degrees. Indoor air temperature is measured five feet above floor. Duct temperature is measured at a register where air enters the house. Early morning is the coldest time of day.

May 2000

May	PM Outside temp	PM Duct temp	PM Indoor temp
1	62	64	69
2	69	69	70
3	75	69	71
4	90	67	74
5	89	69	75
6	70	69	76
7	80	69	75
8	68	70	74
9	73	69	73
10	74	70	75
11	69	69	75
12	54	69	69
13	65	69	69
14	72	69	72
15	74	70	73
16	68	67	72
17	61	69	70
18	65	69	69
19	64	69	70
20	68	70	73
21	68	71	73
22	80	72	74
23	83	69	75
24	80	72	77
25	73	72	78
26	73	73	77
27	73	74	78
28	82	71	76
29	84	72	78
30	85	72	78
31	86	75	80

Figure 6.7 May 2000 late afternoon temperature comparison in Fahrenheit degrees. Outdoor daily high temperatures at the end of May peaked between 96° to 98° F.

that, in turn, cools the house through the following afternoon. The thermal mass of the straw walls also holds the cool of the night air and contributes to keeping the house comfortable the following day. Closing curtains during the heat of the day –a standard passive solar technique–also reduces indoor temperature.

The plans in Figures 6.4 and 6.5 showed the layout of the exterior ducts and inlets, which were placed at two different times. The ductwork was laid two feet below grade under the house after the initial excavation of the site, but before the concrete stem walls were poured. The long exterior duct runs were placed after the outside of the house was finished, but before the installation of any landscaping or drip irrigation. (Figures 6.8, 6.9, 6.10 and 6.11 show the digging and placement of the ducts).

Based on prior experience, the ducts were laid so they would not cross each other either beneath or outside the house. Each bedroom has a duct of its own, as does the hallway. The Great Room/kitchen has four ducts. (The garage is not served by the earth air conditioning; a supplementary cooling system could be installed if the garage is converted into living space.)

Figure 6.8 Digging duct runs.

Figure 6.9 Laying long duct runs.

Figure 6.10 Vertical duct sections.

Figure 6.11 Multiple ducts in the same run.

All eight ducts continue under a central plenum on the south side of the house (Figure 6.12). Although a standard central air conditioning system could be installed in the plenum, which was designed specifically to permit retrofitting, experience has shown it will not be necessary. At the intake end, the ducts lead vertically to the rain-capped inlets seen in Figure 6.13. The drawing in Figure 6.14 shows how the inlets are covered with screening beneath the rain cap to prevent any small animals or insects from entering. Since the duct connections are not tightly sealed, any water that enters will drain out.

The finished ducts are covered with an adjustable floor register to give occupants greater temperature control of their own space. If desired, the ducts can be cleaned every few years by using forced air.

Figure 6.12 Ducts enter the plenum.

Figure 6.13 Rain-capped air inlets.

Figure 6.14 Cross-section of air inlets.

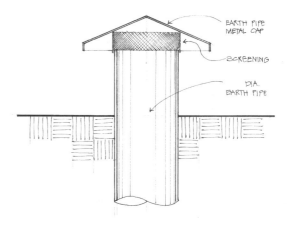

EARTH PIPE METAL CAP

SCREENING

DIA.
EARTH PIPE

EARTH PIPE COVER

Construction: Tin Roof and Roof Ridge Vent

MAY	JUNE	JULY	AUGUST	SEPTEMBER

The "tin" roof is actually corrugated galvanized steel (Figure 6.15) placed over waferboard (OSB) roof decking. The decking (Figure 6.16), which has recycled content, was covered with 30-pound roofing felt to protect the interior of the house shortly after the framing and roof trusses were in place.

Although the metal roof wasn't installed until quite late in the construction cycle of *Casa de Paja*, it could have been placed whenever that the roofers and the materials were available. Just prior to installation of the tin roof, vent holes were cut in the waferboard decking to ensure air access to every curve of the corrugated tin roof. Not only does this yield the best heat escape (through conduction), it also increases air flow and thus improves the efficiency of the earth air conditioning/ heating. The corrugated roofing (Figure 6.17) encourages maximum air movement.

Corrugated metal is the best roofing material for solar

Figure 6.15 Corrugated galvanized steel (tin) roof.

Figure 6.16 Cross-section of roof construction.

Figure 6.17 Close-up of corrugated tin roof.

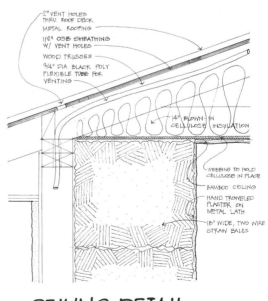

CEILING DETAIL

absorption. Air beneath it gets much hotter than it would under asphalt, tar and gravel, shingles or clay tile. As contradictory as it sounds, the hotter the roof temperature, the stronger the convection currents that draw in cool air, and the more effective the earth air conditioning system. While the non-glare, galvanized roof used on *Casa de Paja* will not rust for a long time, a rusty roof would be an even more effective solar absorber.

Metal roofing meets the sustainable criteria of longevity. Initially a tin roof is more expensive than conventional materials: this roof cost $12,000, about twice as much as a typical roof in New Mexico. However, metal roofing can last up to 75 years with far less maintenance than any other type of roof, which must be replaced every 15 years. The metal and the cellulose insulation in the attic cavity are rated at R-55. The cellulose insulation also absorbs noise from rain or hail.

Along with radiation from the roof, the ridge vents on each section of roof (Figure 6.18) provide the ultimate escape route for heat from the house.

Figure 6.18 Ridge vents are located on each section of the roof.

Construction: A Virtual Cooling Tower

MAY	JUNE	JULY	AUGUST	SEPTEMBER

These vents, together with the master hall vent and the metal roof, act as a chimney or cooling tower. Ancient desert cultures applied the same principal to their minarets and buildings, as seen in Figure 6.19.

The louvered register over the master vent (Figure 6.20) is always open in summer and can be left open in winter, although experience to date shows that is not necessary. Instead, a magnetized cover, placed with a broomstick or other long handle, has been used to halt the airflow. If needed, occupants can use the radiant heating in the floor for additional warmth.

Four ceiling fans located in the bedrooms and Great Room (Figure 6.21) further enhance air circulation; their slanted blades rotate counter-clockwise in the summer to circulate cooling breezes, and clockwise in winter to force warm air down. Outdoor fans on the east portal (Figure 6.22) add a summer breeze.

The utility cost saving is significant. Using a conventional evaporative "swamp" cooler on a house the size of *Casa de Paja* with standard R-30 ceilings and R-11 walls would run about $150 per month at 1999 rates in New Mexico. Refrigerated air conditioning, which is much more efficient in humid weather than an evaporative cooler, would run about $185 per month.

Figure 6.19 Cooling tower on a building in the Middle East. © Corel.

Figure 6.20 Master vent in central hallway.

Similar savings are possible in the winter. Estimated costs for heating Casa de Paja with radiant heat *alone* are estimated at $100-$140 per month. However, with the earth system in place, heating costs have been dramatically lowered, since the air needs to be warmed only a few degrees.

Just as the earth air conditioning system takes advantage of the earth, the sun, and the wind, water harvesting takes advantage of the rain to preserve the planet's precious resources. Let's take a look at this in the next chapter.

Figure 6.21 Indoor ceiling fan.

Figure 6.22 Outdoor ceiling fans under east portal.

Mainstreaming Sustainable Architecture

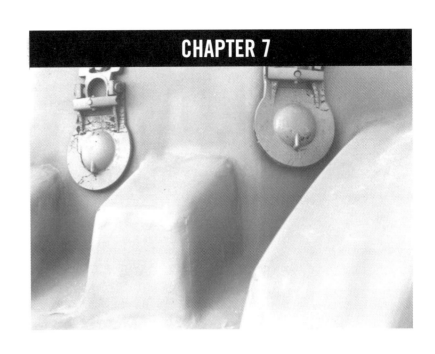

Sustainable Element:

Active Rainwater Harvesting

Rainwater harvesting is defined as the "capture, diversion and storage of water for landscape irrigation and other uses." It can be simple: directing the flow of rainwater down a gutter into a flowerbed (passive collection). Or it can be complex, as it is in *Casa de Paja*, which uses a solar-powered pump to distribute stored water to the drip irrigation system, fountain, and toilets.

Rainwater harvesting is *not* gray-water, which refers to the capture and re-use of water from sinks and tubs for irrigation. It's also important to distinguish rainwater harvesting from xeriscaping—landscaping using plants with low water demand. Rainwater harvesting increases the supply of water; xeriscaping reduces the demand.

Rainwater, which is free of salts and minerals, flushes salts away from the root zone of plants. Consequently the plants themselves demonstrate greater root growth and water uptake, leading to increased drought tolerance. And since rainwater harvesting techniques "sink and spread" water slowly through a landscape, they can alleviate flooding and soil erosion.

Costs Versus Benefits

Rainwater harvesting helps preserve water as a valuable resource by recharging the acquifer, although that is difficult to quantify. It's easier to quantify savings in water utility bills. For instance, in nearby Albuquerque, harvesting rainwater from the roof of an average city home receiving about 11 inches of rainfall per year would generate 13,800 gallons of extra water. Since Albuquerque residents pay 89 cents for each 748 gallons of water, the average 48,000 gallons of water used annually for irrigation alone would cost a household $57. (The average total household consumption is 133,000 gallons per year; irrigation accounts for 36 percent; toilet flushing for up to 40 percent. Some homeowners expend as much as 50 percent of their water on landscaping.)

Like all homes in Corrales, *Casa de Paja* relies on a private well, not on a municipal water system. That makes it tempting to think of the water as "free" after the initial cost of drilling.

However, a falling water table eventually costs not only the environment, but the homeowner as well. It means drilling a deeper well at the rate of $16 per foot! Even property values may decline if water availability is limited.

The hard costs of water acquisition can be calculated for *Casa de Paja*: The well cost $3000 to drill. The pump and installation is amortized over a 10-year period at $20 per month, and it will cost an addition $10 to $25 per month in electricity to run it. (The total monthly cost is roughly comparable to the base cost of water using the city water supply in Albuquerque.)

New trends in pricing for water usage and well permits may encourage homeowners to conserve. As communities recognize that water should be priced based on its value, rather than the immediate cost of acquisition, the commodity cost will ultimately rise. This in turn may raise consciousness about the limited supply of water available in the high desert of New Mexico and many other areas.

Types of Rainwater Harvesting

Passive systems use gutters and simple grading, such as ditches and berms, to capture water and direct it to plants. **Active (or complex) systems** for rainwater collection use storage tanks and forced distribution to retain water for later use, thus smoothing out the time differential between supply and demand.

Complex systems have four parts:
- a **catchment system** for collecting rain from surfaces, including roofs, paving, and soil. The size, surface texture, and slope of the catchment area all affect the amount of water harvested;
- a **conveyance system**, connecting catchment areas to the storage system; in *Casa de Paja*, this is primarily gutters;
- a storage system for holding water; and
- a distribution system to send water where and when it's needed.

Complex systems like the one in *Casa de Paja* yield larger water savings than passive systems, but they do so at the price of higher construction costs. The total system cost for *Casa de Paja* is shown in Figure 7.1. Since payback for rainwater harvesting may take several years, a homeowner's commitment to a "water conservation ethic" is really thrown into high profile. (To be sure, a simple rain barrel collector and gravity-fed irrigation system can be built for as little as $50.)

Figure 7.1 Costs for rainwater harvesting

Rain gutters	$2100
Cistern (1000 gallon)	$ 520
*Plumbing for solar pump and cistern	$ 530
*Solar equipment (panel, pump, switches)	$1500
Total	$4650

* denotes costs for active portion

A Unique Solution for Every House

Every site is unique when it comes to determining the amount of rainwater that can be collected. Both supply and demand fluctuate from year to year depending on the weather and the month in which rain falls. We can calculate whether the supply of rainwater will meet the demand based on "averages," as we'll see below. In reality, there is simply no way to control the reliability of rain.

New Mexico experiences its rainy season from mid-summer through fall. Summer "monsoons" usually hit in the late afternoon, often producing more rain in a short period of time than the landscape can absorb. After the root zone is saturated, water runs off or stands on the surface. On the other hand, winter months may evidence little or no precipitation.

Obviously, the demand for water is greater than average when the weather is hotter than normal. Demand for water also increases while new plants get established and as plants grow

larger. One can reduce demand for water through xeriscaping techniques such as these, which are covered in greater detail in the next chapter:
- reducing the amount of landscaped area
- reducing plant density
- replacing high-water use plants with low-water use plants
- using mulch to reduce surface evaporation.

Reducing demand also reduces the amount of storage needed, thereby reducing the cost of construction. Alternately, one can increase the supply of water by:
- increasing the size of the catchment area or adding new areas
- using more supplemental water
- using the surface techniques described in Chapter 8 to capture runoff from landscape.

Catchment, Collection, and Cistern Considerations

Figure 7.2 diagrams the roof area used for catchment in *Casa de Paja*. Although runoff from the southwest side of the roof is not directed in the cistern, it is captured by the landscape through swales and ponds.

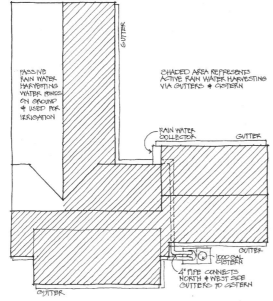

Figure 7.2 Roof catchment areas.

Taking advantage of the slope of the property to move water from roof to storage and from storage to landscaping reduces the amount of pumping needed. *Casa de Paja* is situated on a triangular plot with a slope of 6 percent. The landscape plan in Figure 7.3 shows the location of the well, cistern, and other water harvesting features, all of which take advantage of the natural slope.

The 1000-gallon, above ground cistern seen in Figure 7.4 was placed in an unobtrusive area; it could be further hidden by a screen, trellised vine, or other plants. Underground storage would have been possible, but it's more expensive due to the cost of excavation and soil removal, and the expense of pumping water out. The *Casa de Paja* cistern is opaque, covered, secure from children, and labeled as unfit for drinking. It was painted to reduce the amount of heat absorbed from direct sunlight.

To remove dirt and debris, gutter screens were used on all the downspouts. The dual-compartment cistern design shown in Figure 7.5 reduces the possibility that sediments might clog the irrigation or toilet plumbing. Water enters the left chamber, and then flows around and over a filtering baffle to fill the right chamber, from which water exits to the pump in the garage. Most sediment remains on the bottom right. The entire system can be flushed out with a septic tank vacuum once every 10 years for about $85. The drip system itself includes additional fine filtering screens (200 mesh).

In the event of overflow, the rubber flap valves, seen in the close-up view of Figure 7.6, allow water to run down the outside of the tank into the creek bed in the east courtyard. Alternately, when there is not enough rainfall to fill the cistern to a minimum of seven inches, a float valve triggers automatic filling from the well. A back-flow prevention device prevents any cistern water from flowing back toward the potable water system.

Figure 7.3 Overview of landscape plan for water harvesting.

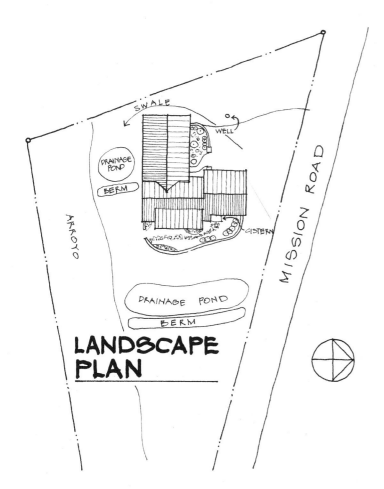

LANDSCAPE
PLAN

Figure 7.4 1,000 gallon, above ground, fiberglass cistern.

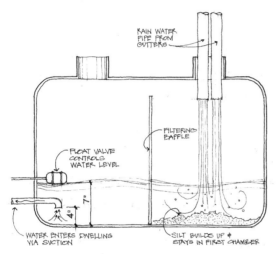

RAIN WATER PIPE FROM GUTTERS

FILTERING BAFFLE

FLOAT VALVE CONTROLS WATER LEVEL

7"

4"

WATER ENTERS DWELLING VIA SUCTION

SILT BUILDS UP & STAYS IN FIRST CHAMBER

CISTERN DETAIL

Figure 7.5 Diagram of dual compartment cistern.

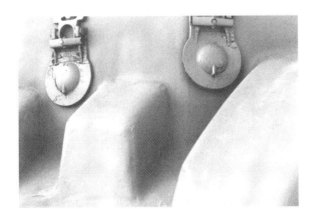

Figure 7.6 Rubber flap valves release overflow.

Distribution Concerns

Casa de Paja faces some unique distribution concerns because of its multi-purpose use of rainwater, as seen in the system diagram in Figure 7.7. An in-line solar pump distributes water to automatic drip irrigation system, the fountain, and the toilets. The pump is pressure-activated: when a valve is opened by flushing or by the timer on the irrigation system, the pressure drops and the pump turns on. Although an inexpensive pump ($85) was used here, a more expensive model ($400) would have been quieter.

Figure 7.7 Diagram of water distribution system.

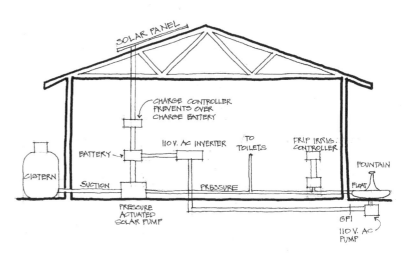

WATER DISTRIBUTION

Harvesting Calculations

In New Mexico, where water supply and demand are not simultaneous, it's especially important to predict how much water storage will be needed and how much water is required to supplement rainwater harvesting. The technique is simple:

- project the monthly water supply (rainfall harvest yield);
- estimate the monthly demand (plant and other water requirements);
- compute the net monthly storage requirement and auxiliary needs.

Yield Calculations

Obviously, the amount of rain received, its duration, and its intensity all affect how much water will be harvested, particularly with passive techniques in which water is collected from catchment areas other than roofs. The timing of rain will also determine how much water the soil will be able to absorb. A single rainstorm may saturate dry soil, but multiple rains may run off because the soil is already wet. (The landscaping techniques described in Chapter 8 capture all the rainwater and pond it to percolate into the ground.)

To manage these calculations, you may need to find a good local source of data. The data used here were originally collected by the City of Albuquerque from the Western Region Climate Control and the National Oceanographic and Atmospheric Administration (NOAA). Similar data may be available for your area from your local county extension service, weather bureau, on-line weather service, or landscape companies.

The amount of water available may surprise you. The rough rule of thumb for calculating runoff from a catchment area is that one inch of rain on one square foot of area will yield 0.6233 gallons. In other words, every 1000 feet of surface yields over 600 gallons of water! The table in Figure 7.8 shows this equivalence from 1 to 15 inches of rain.

Inches rain/year	Gallons/sq ft
1	0.6
2	1.2
3	1.9
4.	2.5
5	3.1
6	3.7
7	4.4
8	5.0
9	5.6
10	6.2
11	6.9
12	7.5
13	8.1
14	8.7
15	9.3

Figure 7.8 Annual water supply available from roof catchment.

To determine the catchment area, simply multiply the length of the roof that is drained times its width; ignore the slope of the roof. Then multiply by the results by 0.623. If you want to be more precise, multiply the result by a runoff coefficient from the table in Figure 7.9. The runoff coefficient indicates the inevitable loss of rain based on evaporation, wind, the type of roofing material used, and inefficiencies in the collection system, such as a gutter that overflows. Use a high coefficient value for a surface that is less absorbent (high water runoff). Use a low coefficient value if you have a more absorbent surface (less runoff).

Figure 7.9 Runoff coefficients © 1999 City of Albuquerque. Used with permission.

Material	High	Low
Roof: Metal, gravel, asphalt, shingle, fiberglass, mineral paper	0.95	0.90
Paving: Concrete, asphalt	1.00	0.90
Gravel	0.70	0.25
Soil: Flat, bare	0.75	0.20
Soil: Flat with vegetation	0.60	0.10
Lawn: Flat, sandy soil	0.10	0.05
Lawn: Flat, heavy soil	0.17	0.13

We do this calculation for *Casa de Paja* by month in Figure 7.10. The catchment area was calculated by assessing the size of the drained areas of the roof.

Even in arid Corrales, New Mexico, there's a substantial amount of rainwater there for the taking!

Figure 7.10 Yield calculation by month for Casa de Paja. Rainfall data © City of Albuquerque. Used with permission.

Yield Calculations for Casa de Paja					
	Rainfall in inches/month per sq ft	Multiply by 0.623 = rainfall in gal/mo	Catchment area in sq ft	Multiply by gal/mo by catchment area for yield	Runoff co-efficient for tin roof	Multiply co-efficient by yield for net yield in gal/mo
January	0.43	0.24	2869	688	0.95	654
February	0.39	0.22	2869	631	0.95	600
March	0.67	0.38	2869	1090	0.95	1036
April	0.65	0.36	2869	1032	0.95	981
May	0.68	0.38	2869	1090	0.95	1036
June	0.82	0.46	2869	1319	0.95	1254
July	1.63	0.91	2869	2610	0.95	2480
August	1.95	1.09	2869	3127	0.95	2971
September	1.18	0.66	2869	1893	0.95	1799
October	0.85	0.48	2869	1377	0.95	1308
November	0.91	0.51	2869	1463	0.95	1390
December	0.64	0.36	2869	1032	0.95	981
Total	10.80	6.05	2869	17357	0.95	16490

Demand Calculations

In most cases, this involves only an estimate of how much water is required for a given landscaped area. As you'll see in Chapter 8, the irrigation demand for *Casa de Paja* varies from summer to winter and decreases after the first year, once plants have become established. The landscaping need shown in the chart is generous. The native plants used at *Casa de Paja* can survive on minimal water in serious drought conditions. Consequently, irrigation needs are lower than the average household.

For *Casa de Paja*, we also needed to estimate the water demand for toilet flushing and fountains. We estimated flushing as follows:

1.6 gal/flush x 20 flushes/day (four people x five flushes) x 30 days = 960 gal/mo.

The fountain water is recycled but must be replenished due to evaporation. Let's assume that the fountain runs automatically for eight hours a day for cooling purposes from May through September. Its 50-gallon capacity is refilled every five days.

All three values are combined in the table in Figure 7.11. For simplicity, we have ignored the other forms of passive

Figure 7.11 Estimated major water demands by month for Casa de Paja after Year 1.

Monthly demand	Landscaping need in gal/mo	Toilet need in gal/mo	Fountain need in gal/mo	Total need in gal/mo
Jan	430	960	0	1390
Feb	430	960	0	1390
Mar	430	960	0	1390
Apr	900	960	0	1860
May	1806	960	300	3066
June	1806	960	300	3066
July	1806	960	300	3066
Aug	1806	960	300	3066
Sept	900	960	300	2160
Oct	430	960	0	1390
Nov	430	960	0	1390
Dec	430	960	0	1390
TOTAL	11604	11,520	1500	24624

rainwater harvesting described in Chapter 8, as well as other minor demands such as laundry, bathing, and dishwashing.

Storage and Auxiliary Supply Calculations

Finally, we compared supply and demand by month. Of course, the amount of water collected and stored will depend on the actual rainfall and usage.

In the chart below, a given month's well water usage is cumulative. When the storage amount for a month is negative, i.e. a month's water demand exceeds the supply of stored water, the amount is added to the Well Water column to indicate how much cumulative supplemental water is needed. Figure 7.12 shows this calculation for *Casa de Paja* by month. Although well water is still needed, it represents only about one-third the total water demand.

As you can see, there may be months when the amount of harvested water (yield) exceeds the capacity of the current cistern. It is not uncommon in New Mexico to find that summer months require a supplemental water supply since so much moisture evaporates in the heat.

Figure 7.12 Storage and cumulative well water use by month for Casa de Paja after Year 1.

Month	Yield from Figure 7.10	Demand from Figure 7.11.	Storage (yield less demand)	Cumulative water use from well
Year 1				
Jan	654	1390	-736	736
Feb	600	1390	-790	1526
Mar	1036	1390	-354	1880
Apr	981	1860	-879	2759
May	1036	3066	-2030	4789
June	1254	3066	-1812	6601
July	2480	3066	-586	7187
Aug	2971	3066	-95	7282
Sept	1799	2160	-361	7643
Oct	1308	1390	-82	7725
Nov	1390	1390	0	7725
Dec	981	1390	-409	8134
TOTAL	16490	24642	-8134	8134

Monitoring and Maintenance

Regular maintenance tasks for the rainwater system will be straightforward:

- keeping gutters and downspouts free of debris;
- flushing debris from the bottom of the cistern once every 10 years;
- cleaning drip irrigation filters regularly.

Now let's turn to the actual construction techniques used in *Casa de Paja*.

Construction: Catchment Areas

MAY	JUNE	JULY	AUGUST	SEPTEMBER

For the purposes of this chapter, the catchment area is defined only as the tin roof. As described above, *Casa de Paja* drains 25 percent of the roof surface directly to the swales and ponds. The driveway and walkways are gently graded to drain into landscape areas. The six percent slope of the plot ensures that runoff from the land in strong rainstorms will be deposited in a holding pond near the east (low) end of the property. From there it gradually seeps into the natural vegetation (un-landscaped portion of the land) and prevents water from flooding the septic leach field or running off the property.

Construction: Conveyance System

MAY	JUNE	JULY	AUGUST	SEPTEMBER

The front plenum and gutters on the east ultimately drain 75 percent of the roof into the cistern. Gutters run along the north wall, across the west-facing kitchen wall, and along the garage into a collection plenum 6"x24"x24" in size (seen in Figure 7.13). The plenum slows the flow of water from gutters into a 4-inch PVC pipe that runs through the garage and the utility room at a slope of 1/4-inch per foot. Since the plenum has no lid, any overflow will simply run out the top.

The gutter collection network on the east side (Figure 7.14) also drains into the cistern, thus making the cistern completely gravity fed. Figure 7.15 shows both systems feeding into the cistern.

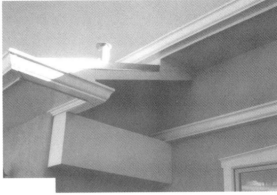

Figure 7.13 Guttering along eaves and collection plenum in front of house.

Figure 7.14 East side gutter collection network.

Figure 7.15 Water from east and front gutters enters cistern.

Construction: Storage System Cistern

MAY	JUNE	JULY	AUGUST	SEPTEMBER	

The 1000-gallon fiberglass cistern is sold as a septic tank. Originally bright yellow, it was painted to match the stucco color so it would blend into the house. The cistern is situated in a corner that is invisible from the interior of the house or from the street. Since this 1000-gallon tank weighs 8500 pounds when full, a 4-inch concrete pad was poured before the cistern was installed.

At a cost of $520, the cost per gallon for storage was about 50 cents. Typical 55-gallon barrels used for passive rainwater collection cost about $10-$50. The float valve is set to add well water to the tank whenever the level sinks to a minimum level of seven inches.

Construction: Distribution System

MAY	JUNE	JULY	AUGUST	SEPTEMBER	

Figure 7.16 Roof-top solar collector

As mentioned above, a solar pump distributes non-potable rainwater to the drip irrigation system, the toilets, and the fountain in the north courtyard. (All drinking water comes from the well.)

A 1/20th hp, 12V water pump with a pressure switch pumps water from the cistern into the rainwater piping on demand. When a toilet is flushed, the fountain turned on, or the automatic drip system activated, the pressure drops and the pump turns on. The pump itself is powered by a rooftop solar collector (Figure 7.16) that charges its recyclable 12-volt battery. Solar-powered pumps have a reliable record of working in all climates and weather.

It is possible to switch the toilet system completely to well water simply by turning two valves in the garage. The two low-flow toilets use only 1.6 gallons per flush. The pump, battery, and distribution system are located in the garage, as seen in Figure 7.17.

Figure 7.17 Distribution system in the garage.

Construction: Primary Water Source

MAY	JUNE	JULY	AUGUST	SEPTEMBER
■				

The private well was drilled to 300 feet over two-and-a-half days. The geological formation in the area made it easy to drill; the pipe was sunk through several clay lenses, which separate strata of water. Large pumps placed at the bottom of a well can produce water at a potential rate of up to 40 gallons per minute. In *Casa de Paja*, a 10 gallon-per-minute pump is used, well above the state minimum of four gallons per minute. As a matter of standard maintenance, the submersible pump must be replaced every seven to 10 years at an estimated cost of $600 to $850.

A concrete pad around the wellhead seals the casing at the top, leaving about 18 inches of well casing above ground on the west side of the house. (See Figure 7.18.) A water softener to remove naturally occurring iron and other minerals may be installed in the garage.

We've now looked at the primary water supply and the active rainwater harvesting system. Now let's turn to passive rainwater harvesting techniques and xeriscaping as we explore the role of landscaping in the creation of a sustainable house.

Figure 7.18 Well casing on the west side of house.

CHAPTER 8

Mainstreaming Sustainable Architecture

Sustainable Elements:

Xeriscaping and Passive Water Distribution

Landscaping for the desert involves more than the selection of plants with low-to-medium water requirements (xeriscaping). Other elements include:

- energy-efficiency
- grouping plants with similar water requirements
- land contouring and drainage
- irrigation techniques
- creeks, courtyards, and fountains.

Well-selected plants and trees contribute to energy efficiency by providing shade in the summer and permitting more sun to enter the house in winter. Plants absorb some of the sun's energy, thus lowering the air temperature immediately outside the house and reducing the need for cooling. Subdivision rules limit the use of large deciduous trees at *Casa de Paja*; they preclude trees over 12 feet tall lest they interfere with the views prized by other homeowners.

Appropriate land contouring and drainage not only minimize the use of water from the acquifer, they also constrain erosion. In Corrales, where homeowners can be fined for rainwater running off their property, it's essential to have a landscape design that harvests rainwater from the land surface, diverts it through berms (like speed bumps), channels into ponding areas, and stores it to eliminate runoff.

Compared to sprinkler heads, a buried drip irrigation system reduces the loss of water by evaporation and loss from watering more area than necessary. It delivers water exactly where it's needed. In the case of *Casa de Paja*, irrigation water is supplied primarily by active rainwater harvesting, while passive techniques help lower the overall amount of water required.

Finally, courtyards, creek beds and fountains can be used to create "micro-climates" that channel breezes while blocking heavy winds. These features increase humidity near the house, while offering psychological relief from summer heat. This chapter will look at land contouring, irrigation techniques, micro-climates, and xeriscaping at *Casa de Paja*.

Planting with Purpose

In addition to shading, plants soften the micro-climate around a desert house like *Casa de Paja* in many ways. They release water vapor to provide evaporative cooling, reduce glare, provide privacy, slow the wind (which can gust to 70 mph in Corrales), and trap blowing dust that would otherwise enter the house. Screening by trees, plants, or hedges is particularly desirable on the windward side of a house, as well as on the sun-beaten east and west sides.

The right vegetation can lower the temperature around a house by as much as 14° F (8° C). Some xeric plants, like cacti, literally absorb large amounts of solar radiation. A vine climbing a trellis in front of an east or west wall not only insulates against the summer sun (especially if combined with additional layers of trees and shrubs), but can increase the life expectancy of a building by slowing the inevitable processes of corrosion, discoloration, or cracking. A dense ground cover reduces the reflection of heat and light compared to pavement, while preventing erosion and trapping water runoff.

Planting Principles

A few guidelines, useful everywhere, directed the selection and placement of plants at *Casa de Paja*:

- Plants and water drainage systems were placed to assist each other. Gravity-fed water from any cistern overflow will water plants near the creek bed; earth berms trap water near trees for slow root watering.
- Various plants perform functions besides decor, acting as windbreak, shade, mulch, erosion control, wildlife (bird) habitat, temperature buffer, humidity source, or soil conditioner. In other circumstances, possible plant uses might also include privacy, food, camouflage, forage, fuel, fire protection, or insect repellent.
- Each important function is handled by multiple methods. For instance, water is caught in a variety of ways besides harvesting from the roof.

- Planting is done by zone, according to how much water plants will need.
- Wells or "waffle iron" settings for individual plants not only trap water, but provide a catch basin for mulch and debris that blows across the site.

Passive Water Collection

A similar set of principles guided the placement of passive water collection systems. Water diversion and storage is important everywhere, not just in the desert. Thin sheets of runoff water, which generally appear after less than an inch of rain, can be trapped, diverted, or stored to help recharge the groundwater and reduce erosion. New Mexico is not alone with its over-drawn aquifers; water that is captured and returned to the water table benefits the earth even if it doesn't directly benefit the homeowner. Remember, it doesn't take much slope to change the flow of water.

Swales are long excavations that capture and direct water flow into ponding areas. Traditional swales, built on contour or level survey lines, intercept water runoff and hold it for a few hours or days until it seeps into the soil or is picked up by vegetation. In less sandy soils, the bottom of a swale is generally covered with gravel, sand, or loosened soil to facilitate holding water.

Holding ponds store water that overflows from swales. Given the need to handle intermittent heavy rains at *Casa de Paja*, the swales direct water from upslope areas to downslope holding ponds, which are just large shallow depressions in the earth. The sandy soil of Corrales is so porous—almost like sugar—that the water soaks fairly quickly into the ground. Shallow ponds like these usually harvest a runoff area about 20 times their size.

Without the ponds, there would be no safe overflow during monsoon rains; rushing water could quickly erode the land into gullies. In other soil situations or climates, the "pond" effect can be achieved with native grasses, gravel, stone spillways, or stepped terraces. More permanent storage basins can be built of earth, stone, concrete, or the water can be piped into an underground storage tank for later use in irrigation.

Berms are small, crescent-shaped earth dams that catch water running down a slope or off a roof. They are often used around trees and shrubs to hold run-off until it can sink into the ground. If used to trap roof water, grading and berms should be created in such a way that water is held more than 5 feet from the foundation. A spillway can be constructed in a berm to direct overflow where needed.

Construction: Land Contouring

MAY	JUNE	JULY	AUGUST	SEPTEMBER	
				■	

Land contouring was executed by grading to ensure large-scale drainage from the land, small-scale drainage from hard surfaces, and individual water harvesting features.

Large-scale contouring took place when the lot was originally graded for the house to take into account the slope of the land. Runoff swales were dug during final grading along the west and south sides of the house (Figure 8.1). The swales will eventually display native, un-watered plants like chamisa.

Figure 8.1 Large-scale land contouring appears on the landscape plan.

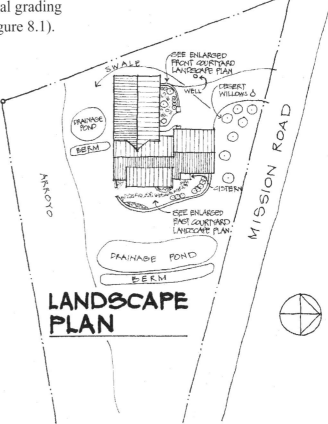

LANDSCAPE PLAN

Figure 8.2 Drainage ditches parallel
the road opposite the house.

Figure 8.3 Grading assured the capture
of rain water from the driveway.

The swales direct the flow of water from the north and west sides of the property away from the foundation of the house and toward two shallow depressions (ponding areas). One is located in the southwest corner of the property and another on the narrow, east end. Taken together, the contouring features have an estimated capacity of 3000 cubic feet (100 feet x 300 feet x 1 foot depth) or 21,600 gallons of water. Between the swales and the ponds, the drainage system can accommodate the runoff from two inches of rainfall on hard-packed dirt or when the ground is saturated after multiple rainstorms. (Two inches of rain has a potential runoff of 1.33 inches.)

To catch roadway runoff, the Village of Corrales requires bar ditches running parallel to the road, as seen in Figure 8.2. Since the street by *Casa de Paja* slopes to the north, the ditches are located on the opposite side of the street. A house situated on that side might be able to divert some water from the drainage ditch to its own pond for later watering.

Grading also assured the capture of rainwater from all hard surfaces. For instance, the driveway slopes slightly to both the north (directing runoff to trees) and to the west, directing runoff into the swale that drains to the southwest ponding area (see Figure 8.3). The bricked entry path slopes toward planted areas on either side, while runoff from the brick floor of the east portal empties into the creek bed. (See Figures 8.4 and 8.5.) The bricks are not set in concrete, so water can also drain between them.

The creek bed, now filled with decorative landscape rocks (see Figure 8.6), was dug after all exterior construction was complete. Created to capture runoff from the east portal and overflow from the water cistern, the creek bed ultimately empties into one of the drainage ponds. It "disappears" beneath the eastern wall of the courtyard, as shown in the cross-section diagram of Figure 8.7, but actually continues to flow in a swale to the ponding area to the east. As the calculations in Chapter 7 showed, it is conceivable that the creek will contain visible water during July and August, the months when heavy rainstorms could exceed the capacity of the cistern.

Figure 8.4 The brick path in the front courtyard slopes toward planted areas.

Figure 8.6 The creek bed filled with decorative landscape rocks.

Figure 8.5 Runoff from the brick floor of the east portal drains into the creek bed.

*Figure 8.7 Cross-section of
creek bed flowing underground
beneath the courtyard wall.*

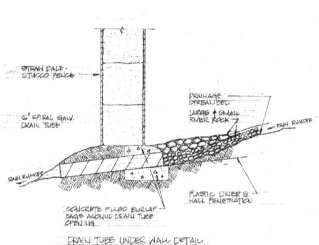

DRAIN TUBE UNDER WALL DETAIL

*Figure 8.8 Large rocks on the north side
serve a decorative purpose, but also
trap or slow water runoff.*

Large rocks (shown in Figure 8.8) were placed on the north side of the house, both for decorative purposes and to trap or slow down surface water. Berms around each tree on the north side of the house also trap water.

Each of the small and medium-sized plants was placed in an individual circular well that will hold rainwater long enough for it to be absorbed into the soil. Since the plant beds in both courtyards were later covered with 3/4-inch brown, Santa Fe Deco Stone two inches deep, the small wells are barely visible in Figure 8.9.

The landscaper placed a fabric landscape mat (Typar®) beneath the gravel in both courtyards. The mat acts as a mulch,

*Figure 8.9 A circular well around
each plant is mulched with gravel.*

letting moisture in. However, the fabric maintains a more consistent ground temperature than other mulches, slows evaporation, and helps with weed management. Any form of mulch can cover this fabric. Stone was selected for *Casa de Paja* for its ease of maintenance (it doesn't blow away, float, or fade) and to enhance the Southwest feel.

Construction: Drip Irrigation

MAY	JUNE	JULY	AUGUST	SEPTEMBER

As described in the previous chapter, the drip irrigation system draws water from the cistern. While the detailed elements of the irrigation system diagrammed in Figure 8.10 were placed after exterior construction, one important feature was incorporated during plumbing rough-out: a pipe taps water from the solar-powered cistern pump in the garage to bring water to the north side of the house and the fountain. This pressure-activated pump turns on as soon as the pressure drops in the system. At the same time, plumbing was incorporated for a hose bib on each side of the house.

The automatic timer in the garage is set to water 20 minutes a day in summer and 10 minutes twice a week in winter. This abbreviated time is sufficient since the reliability of water is more important than its volume. The system, gauged at a flow of five gallons per minute, delivers 100 gallons per summer day or 700 gallons per week.

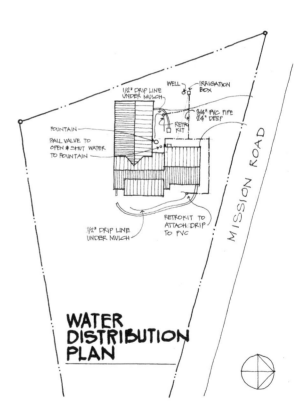

Figure 8.10 Irrigation system diagram.

This translates into roughly 2.5 gallons of water per week for each of 277 plants, as shown in Figure 8.11.

This is more than enough during the first crucial year when plants require extra water to become established. (All plants were computed as medium usage, although they represent a mix of low- and medium-water use.)

Figure 8.11 Estimated plant water requirements to calculate water needs.

Type of Plant	First Year	After Established
Low Water Use Plants	1.5 gal/wk	1.0 gal/wk
Medium Water Use Plants	2.5 gal/wk	1.5 gal/wk
High Water Use Plants	>3.0 gal/wk	>2.0 gal/wk

Drip irrigation systems can easily be expanded to accommodate future plantings by adding additional 1/4-inch tubes. Although *Casa de Paja* uses a solar-powered pump to generate pressure for irrigation, a gravity-fed system on the east side of the house could have been effective with a drop of merely 1/8-inch per foot.

After the first year, summer water use can be scaled back by experience, perhaps to 12-13 minutes a day. The desert willow trees on the north side should survive well on natural rainfall and runoff after the first year. The drip tubes for these trees then can be capped off and moved elsewhere if needed.

Construction: Courtyard Micro-climates

The two shaded, planted courtyards serve multiple purposes. They:

- add shade against the rising and setting sun;
- protect the house from winds that can gust to 70 mph in spring;
- reduce the nuisance of blowing sand that affects every house in the desert Southwest;
- offer privacy from the street, automobiles, and neighbors;
- offer psychological "comfort" zones during hot days;
- raise humidity in the area immediately near the house.

The median humidity in Corrales is only 20 percent; days with a humidity over 50 percent are rare, usually occurring only a few times during the summer monsoon season. Higher humidity adds significantly to the comfort level of the house. Evaporation from the concrete fountain (see Figure 8.12) in the north courtyard is expected to raise the courtyard humidity by 20 percent. The same pipe that feeds the drip system on the north side also feeds the fountain. The pressure-demand pump has a separate shut-off valve for the fountain, which does not run in the winter, when the weather is cold enough for water to freeze and crack the concrete. The fountain offers the soothing and refreshing sound of water, while enhancing the appeal of the front entry.

Figure 8.12 Evaporation from the fountain in the north courtyard is expected to raise the courtyard humidity by 20 percent.

Construction: Xeriscape Planting

MAY	JUNE	JULY	AUGUST	SEPTEMBER

The landscape was "zoned" by plant type into areas with medium water consumption and those with low water. Plants outside the courtyard are low water, native foliage, well adapted to live solely on rainfall after they become established in the first year.

Figures 8.13 and 8.14 show plant detail for the front (north) and east courtyards respectively. The Appendices include a detailed list of the plants, including their water requirements and scientific names. For the most part, the plants used in the courtyards are low maintenance, as well as low water. They require only minimal pruning, pest control, and the annual removal of dead leaves, branches, and blossoms as they mature.

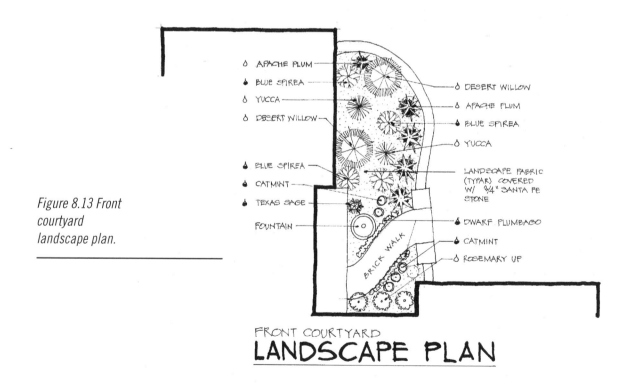

Figure 8.13 Front courtyard landscape plan.

FRONT COURTYARD
LANDSCAPE PLAN

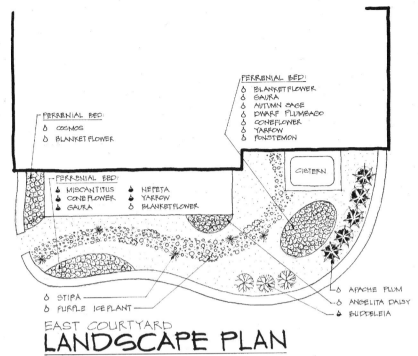

Figure 8.14 East courtyard landscape plan.

PERRENIAL BED:
ᵟ BLANKET FLOWER
ᵟ GAURA
ᵟ AUTUMN SAGE
ᵟ DWARF PLUMBAGO
ᵟ CONEFLOWER
ᵟ YARROW
ᵟ PONSTEMON

PERRENIAL BED:
ᵟ COSMOS
ᵟ BLANKET FLOWER

CISTERN

PERRENIAL BED:
ᵟ MISCANTITUS   ᵟ NEPETA
ᵟ CONE FLOWER   ᵟ YARROW
ᵟ GAURA   ᵟ BLANKET FLOWER

ᵟ STIPA
ᵟ PURPLE ICE PLANT

ᵟ APACHE PLUM
ᵟ ANGELITA DAISY
ᵟ BUDDELEIA

EAST COURTYARD
LANDSCAPE PLAN

Future Landscaping Options

For additional energy efficiency, the homeowners may elect to put deciduous trees (ones that shed their leaves in winter) or shrubs along the south side of the house. Boston ivy could also be planted around the plenum where the cooling ducts enter and around the eight air inlets. The evaporative cooling from the ivy will help cool the air and add humidity. Plants in those locations would also:

- shade the ground around the inlets;
- increase energy efficiency by absorbing solar energy that might otherwise heat the house during the summer;
- take advantage of passive rainwater collection around the plenum from the one portion of the roof that doesn't feed into the cistern; this could be made even more effective with a small swale parallel to the house, or by putting an earth berm by each tree or shrub.

Additional plants (e.g., more Boston ivy) could be added to the north (garage) side of the house, which faces the street, or used to hide the well casing. Climbing vines appropriate for the high desert, such as honeysuckle, could climb a trellis in front of the cistern for camouflage. Vines could also be used to break up and insulate the surface of the west wall. It's easy to bring water to any of these locations simply by running 1/2-inch drip tubing from existing lines now buried six to eight inches underground.

For added color, homeowners could add pansies (in winter) or other annuals to large, hand-watered pots under the portals.

Conclusion

From inside to out, from top to bottom, we have seen that *Casa de Paja* incorporates sustainable principles. The true test, however, comes not in theory, but in practice. *Casa de Paja* is now in the hands of its owners, who have continued to monitor energy usage and air temperature from the cooling ducts, as well as the efficacy of rainwater harvesting. In the Epilog, we'll learn about their experience of living in the house, the surprises they've encountered and the changes they plan.

EPILOG

Arab Proverb:

The secret is in the people who live in the house and not in the house itself.

It's not clear whether Virginia Price and Allen Heaton bought *Casa de Paja*, or whether the house bought them. Long interested in environmentalism, the retired couple had already lived in a tin-roofed, solar envelope house in Pagosa Springs, Colorado. (A solar envelope is an energy efficient, but expensive method of double-walled construction that enhances passive solar collection). And they spent several years living in a flat-roofed adobe in Mountainair, New Mexico, about 60 miles southeast of Albuquerque, where they harvested rainwater for irrigating their land and watering their animals. As Allen admits, "We're probably more open to these things than some other people."

"I'd be willing to do my part..."

When they decided to move to the Albuquerque area in late 1999, the couple was already thinking about their next environmental challenge. "We looked at straw bale houses, tire houses. There was always the feeling that I'd be willing to do my part," says Virginia. "But this is elegant! I never thought that we would be living in a house with so many environmental features and still feel that it's so luxurious."

Their friends are equally surprised that *Casa de Paja* "is not some straw bale hovel with plaster globbed on the walls as we all felt these homes had to be," she reports. She explains that friends arrive with an indulgently supportive attitude: "Isn't that nice, they bought a straw bale house and they're going to do their part to save the world, da-dah, da-dah, da-dah. Then they walk in and they're just amazed."

What their friends didn't expect was a house that incorporated so many sustainable features without compromising design. Even to Virginia and Allen, many of the sustainable elements were new. To be sure, they already understood how to orient a house for passive solar heating. Certainly they knew about water conservation, having collected 125 gallons of rainwater in barrels in Mountainair, but they didn't have rainwater plumbed into the house. "That's amazing, the whole concept of using rainwater to flush toilets," adds Virginia.

Homeowners Virginia Price and Allen Heaton.

And they've found a special value to the linseed-oil-finished, hand-plastered walls. Allen almost apologizes that they haven't hung paintings or photos on the walls, even several months after moving in. "The walls are wonderful. That's part of the reason we bought the house," he says. Virginia finds the walls "alive." "Throughout the day, the light changes and I'll see something different in the texture."

"We lost our hearts..."

It's clear that Virginia and Allen have a strong emotional response to *Casa de Paja*. From the very first time they saw the house on Thanksgiving weekend 1999, they "lost their hearts."

Allen says that the thick walls gave the house "a warm feeling, a comfortable feeling, a safe feeling. It's very nurturing." Even small things, such as a hallway designed with angles and offset doors, add interest to the design. Another joy comes from the expansive views. Daytime offers the Sandia Mountains and the bosque; night brings the city lights of Albuquerque.

The biggest surprises, however, came in less visible ways. First, they feel that the air quality has improved their health. Allen compares it to the double-insulated solar envelope house, in which air quickly became stale unless the windows were opened. The air in *Casa de Paja*, which changes completely every two hours, always seems fresh. In spite of the rate of air exchange, the couple hasn't felt any drafts.

"I'm surprised we can heat this volume of space (with natural air flow) and keep it comfortable," Allen says, "especially with high ceilings." Even during the three coldest winter months (January-March), they turned on the heat only half a dozen times. (Please see the temperature charts in Chapter 6.) The house, Allen reports, generally remains a very comfortable 66°-67°, whereas their adobe stayed cold in the winter without constant heating. "For people like us who are retired, long-term energy cost is important. Instead of spending $200 to $300 per month for energy, we've got some savings," he notes. (Their monthly gas bills have averaged less than $40, including the hot water heater and gas clothes dryer.)

Perhaps because the high ceilings consist of bamboo and cellulose instead of plaster, they absorb more noise than anticipated. Virginia is specific. "We can look out the window and see things blowing by so we know the wind is blowing. And I can get under a skylight and hear the rain. But if you're not looking out a window or you're not near a skylight, you don't know."

"A thousand gallons just like that!"

The rate of rainwater collection has been another surprise. The first (and as it turns out, only) rainstorm of their first winter completely filled the storage tank. "It's like the water truck came down the street and said, oh by the way, would you like a thousand gallons of water?" Virginia exclaims. Another day of rain would have added another 500 gallons and resulted in a running creek in the east courtyard. The full tank held enough for 600-700 flushes.

Allen believes the water shortage problem in New Mexico would be greatly alleviated if everyone harvested rainwater, even if they did nothing but hook up the garden hose to a collection barrel. He extends this principle to the use of recycled materials in *Casa de Paja*. "If more builders and contractors would do that, it would really cut down on our energy use in this country."

The couple agree that maintaining design standards eliminated any sense of deprivation. "*Casa de Paja* has an elegance about it. This type of design," they suggest, "is probably the best way of attracting people to sustainable thinking, rather than demanding that buyers sacrifice."

What's behind, what's next

The couple reports having a minor problem obtaining home insurance from one company that refuses to insure straw bale houses. However, four or five other companies said "yes" immediately; it was just a matter of shopping around. They had absolutely no resistance from their lender.

Given the success of the natural air flow system for heating and cooling, Ed Paschich says he'd like to experiment in the company's next straw bale house with using heating coils in each air duct instead of radiant floor heat. By making each duct a separate heating zone, including two separate zones for the master bedroom and master bath, residents would have complete control of interior temperature.

Allen and Virginia plan very few changes. Perhaps they'll put dimmers on the light switches or add greenery around the air inlets to increase humidity. And, of course, place large clay pots of colorful flowers on the patios. "We're very happy here. *Casa de Paja* is a lovely environment for living—much more than just a house!"

GLOSSARY

A
Adze: An axlike tool with a curved blade at right angles to the handle used for dressing wood

Aquifer: A large water-bearing rock formation or group of rock formations

Arroyo: A dry gulch or deep gully

Autoclaved Cellular Cement: A new cement product that reduces energy consumption and solid waste through the re-use of fly ash (a by-product in the production of concrete)

B
Baling Needle: A tool used to reposition the wire tires on straw bales and allow for retying

Berms: Shallow earth dams that hold water in a desired location

Boron: A naturally occurring chemical element used as a pesticide and fire retardant

Bosque: Wooded, river bottomland

Built Environment: Any man-made construction

C
Calcining: To heat to a high temperature causing a loss of moisture, reduction, or oxidation

Cantera: Naturally occurring soft stone popular for carving in Mexico

Casa de Paja: House of straw (Spanish)

Catchment: A direct structure for collecting water

Cellulose: Recycled newspaper

Conduction: The transfer of heat through materials

Convection current: The movement of air caused by a temperature differential

G
Gray Water: The capture and re-use of water from sinks, showers, and washing machines, for irrigation Water from toilets or sinks with garbage disposals is not considered gray water

Green Builder: A builder who uses sustainable architecture and materials that can be maintained long-term without exhausting non-renewable resources

K
Kiva: A rounded, adobe corner fireplace

L
Latillas: Narrow, peeled saplings of small diameter that criss-cross beams to create a ceiling

Life Cycle Inventory (LCI): A measure that provides a quantitative rating for comparing materials, products, and construction methods

M
Malqaf: A shaft extending high above a building to catch the prevailing wind and channel it into the building for cooling effect

Multiple Chemical Sensitivities (MCS): The complex allergic reaction pattern of people to chemicals, especially petroleum products

O

Oriented Strand Board: (waferboard)	Construction product with a high content of recycled wood chips and small diameter, preferably tree-farmed, lumber

P

Plenum:	An air-filled space that receives air for distribution
Ponding:	Preventing rapid runoff and erosion by holding water and allowing it to seep into the ground
Portal:	A covered porch or entryway

R

Rainwater Harvesting:	The capture, diversion, and storage of rainwater for landscape irrigation and other uses
Rebar:	Ridged steel rods for increasing the strength of concrete
Riparian:	Refers to the ecosystems on the wooded bank of a river

S

Salsabil:	A flat marble plate tilted against a wall with water trickling over its surface
Saltillo Tile:	Handmade, low impact clay floor tile from Mexico; unglazed, low temperature fired, and softer than ceramic tile
Soffit:	The underside of the eaves on a house
Stem wall:	Steel reinforced concrete walls that extend from six inches above ground to the top of the foundation
Swales:	Shallow ditches sometimes filled with gravel to increase water absorption

T

Talavera tile:	Handmade, low impact, decorative clay tile from Mexico that is low temperature fired
Travertine:	Naturally occurring stone cut and polished for tile application

V

Vernacular Architecture:	The use of local materials and building design, generally from non-professional builders
Vigas:	Tree trunks with bark removed used as roof beams
Volatile Organic Compounds (VOC)	Carbon-based (organic) compounds that vaporize or evaporate at room temperature, such as paint thinner

X

Xeriscaping:	Landscaping with native plants that have minimal water needs

Straw Bale Houses

Build It With Bales, MacDonald, S.O., et al. InHabitation Services, Gila, NM and Out On Bale, Tucson, AZ: 1994.

The Straw Bale House, Steen, Athena and Bill, et.al. Chelsea Green, White River Junction, VT: 1994.

The Canelo Project, c/o Athena and Bill Steen, HCL Box 324, Elgin, AZ 85611, t: 520-455-5548.

Out on Bale Magazine, 1037 E. Linden St., Tucson, AZ 85719.

The Last Straw: Journal of Straw Bale and Natural Building, HC 66, Box 119, Hillsboro, NM 88042, $28/year U.S., t: 505-895-5400, f: 505-895-3326, e: thelaststraw@strawhomes.com, *http://www.strawhomes.com*

Building With Straw, 3-video series, and other publications, Black Range Films, Natural Building Resources, Star Rt 2, Box 119, Kingston, NM 88042, t: 505-895-5652, f: 505-895-3326, e: resources@StrawBaleCentral.com, *http://www.StrawBaleCentral.com*

Greenbuilding

E Build Library - An Encyclopedic Green Building Reference, a CD-ROM from Environmental Building News and E Build, Inc. Brattleboro, VT: 1998.

Green Builder Program, Home Builders Association of Central New Mexico, 5931 Office Boulevard NE, Suite 2, Albuquerque, NM 87109, t: 505/344-3294.

Rainwater Harvesting

Rainwater Harvesting: Supply from the Sky, City of Albuquerque, NM: 1999.

Texas Guide to Rainwater Harvesting, 2nd ed. Price-Todd, Wendy and Vittori, Gail, Texas Water Development Board, Austin, TX: 1997.

Rainwater Collection for the Mechanically Challenged, Banks, Suzy and Heinichen, Richard, Tank Town Publishing, Dripping Springs, TX: 1997.

American Rainwater Catchment Systems Association, P.O. Box 685283, Austin, TX 78768-5283.

Miscellaneous

Alternative Construction: Contemporary Natural Building Methods, Lynne, Elizabeth, and Adams, Cassandra, eds. Wiley, New York, NY: 2000.

The Natural House Book, Pearson, David. Simon and Schuster, New York: 1989.

_ph.#_ _passage Construction, Corrales, NM._
_898-6284_

Lewis Hyman Inc.
860 East Sand Hill Ave.
Carson, CA 90746
310-532-5700
www.lewishymaninc.com

Boiled Linseed Oil
Hanley/KWAL/Howells Paint
6200 Coors Rd. NE, Ste G-01
Albuquerque, NM 87120
505-898-6094
www.kwal-howells.com

_1800888_
4VWR

Boron
Van Water & Rogers
3301 Edmungs SE
Albuquerque, NM 87102
505-842-6303
www.pestweb.com or _www.vwr-inc.com_

no longer
has Boron

_(425)_
_8935654_

Cistern (septic tank container)
Southwest Piping Supplies
7928 Edith Blvd. NE
Albuquerque, NM 87113
505-898-7473

Engineered Straw Bales
Village Mercantile
3923 Corrales Rd.
Corrales, NM 87048
505-897-9328

Hand-Adzed Ceiling Beams
Adobe Building Supply
P.O. Box 91943
Albuquerque, NM 87199
505-828-9800
www.abslumber.com

Low VOC Paint (Velvasheen)
Hanley/KWAL/Howells Paint
6200 Coors Rd. NE, Ste G-01
Albuquerque, NM 87120
505-898-6094
www.kwal-howells.com

RedTop and Structolite
Hope Stucco & Supply
4200 2nd St. NW
Albuquerque, NM 87107
505-345-1755
www.hopelmbr.com

Saltillo Tile
Saltillo Tile Company
2601 Vassar Dr. NE
Albuquerque, NM 87107
505-881-8669
www.saltillotileco.com

Solar Collector
Direct Power & Water Corp.
4000-B Vassar Dr. NE
Albuquerque, NM 87107
800-260-3792
www.directpower.com

Thermoform Blow-In Insulation and Webbing Mesh
Applegate/Thermocon
2500 Jackson St.
Monroe, LA 71202
800-532-6145 (Delbert Foss)
www.thermocon.com

Undeground AC Ducts (8-inch pipe)
Sigler & Reeves
3330 Pan American Frwy NE
Albuquerque, NM 87107
505-881-2929
www.sigler.com

Contractors Heating & Supply
3501 Princeton NE
Albuquerque, NM 87107
505-884-1460

PLANT LIST

COMMON NAME	BOTANICAL NAME	WATER NEEDS	TYPE
Apache Plume	Fallugia Paradoxa	Low	E. Shrub
Autumn Sage	Salvia greggi	Medium	E. Shrub
Blanket Flower	Gaillardia	Medium	D. Perennial
Blue Mist Spirea	Caryopteris x Clandonensis	Medium	D. Shrub
Catmint	Nepeta mussini	Medium	D. Perennial
Cholla	Opuntia	Low	E. Cactus
Cone Flower	Echinacea Purpurea	Medium	D. Perennial
Cosmos	Cosmos "sensation"	Medium	Annual
Desert Willow	Chilopsis linearsis	Low	Tree
Gaura	Gaura lindheimeri	Medium	D. Perennial
Miscanthus	Miscanthus sinensis	Medium	Grass
Penstmon	Penstemon pinifolius	Low+	E. Perennial
Texas Sage	Leucophyllum frutexcens	Medium	E. Shrub
Up. Rosemary	Romarinus officinalis	Low+	E. Shrub
Yarrow	Achillea millefolium	Medium	E. Perennial
Yucca soft leaf	Yucca pendula	Low+	E. Shrub

INDEX